The Shocking History of the Jesuits (The Society of Jesus)

James Battell

Published by James Battell, 2024.

Also by James Battell

The Shocking History of the Jesuits (The Society of Jesus)
King James I of England: The King The Vatican Could Not Kill
Oliver Cromwell: The Last King of England
The Hidden Truth About Freemasonry, The Catholic Church, And The Illuminati
Bible Prophecy Made Simple For Serious Students of Scripture
Did The Catholic Church Order Abraham Lincoln's Assassination?
Is Calvinism And The Doctrines of Grace Biblical?
The Book of Genesis Commentary (Chapters 1-11)
Watchman Nee, Witness Lee, and Living Stream Ministry: A Critical Analysis of Their Identity as Cult or Church
What Is Speaking In Tongues And Is It Still For Today?
Ephesians Bible Commentary
The Book of Romans Commentary

Chapter 1: "Doctors of Deception and Disguise"

<hr>

I suspect that the Jesuits are rather akin to the Roman Catholic churches' dedicated loyal jihadists, and unlike the present Islamists who clutch the Quran for substance as they wade into battle, the Jesuits follow the teachings of "General" Ignatius Loyola but without the strapped-on shirt bombs of course. Instead, they skillfully use another form of ammunition in their mission to continue rebuilding that old corrupt 'holy' Roman Empire yet again.

Founded in 1540 AD by a Spanish ex-mercenary from the Basque Country, Ignatius of Loyola, they were originally named "the company of Jesus" (a blasphemous title), but it seems the pope of the day did not appreciate the military connotation of the order and instead it was renamed "the Society of Jesus" (just as bad, I know). After all, Loyola had modelled them originally on the Knights Templar, and he may also have been an honouree knight himself (who knows?). According to Baigent and Leigh, however, "Like the Templars, the Jesuits were normally subject only to the [Catholic] church; but like the Templars, they often became a law unto themselves."

Ignatius Loyola, Jesuit founder

The author Edmond Parris writes of Loyola, saying: "That he was a first class example of that active mysticism and distortion of the will...and did not the Madonna herself appear to him one night holding in her arms the child Jesus...he was praying with long fasts, flagellating himself, practicing all forms of maceration, and he even witnessed a serpent's head with many eyes; this it seems gave him much delight but left him depressed when it vanished."

It seems to me that this apparition, or whatever it was, had beguiled this sick man, or maybe he was hallucinating after dabbling with drugs, black magic, or perhaps both.

I have long been aware of the Jesuits' machinations and duplicity against born-again Bible believers and their rubbishing of the spiritual supremacy and authority of the AV, the King James Bible that they so wish to destroy or rewrite. Yet Revelation 22:18-19 is very clear, with a solemn warning to those who dare interferes with this Book or dumbs it down: Don't do it!

They have been warned, and not by us, but by Almighty God!

The Jesuits have been popularly referred to as the "shock troops" of the Catholic church, and even old Joe Stalin – who knew a thing or two – could say accusingly through thick pipe smoke to a blinking Churchill: "The pope! How many divisions has he got?" Was he referring to the Jesuits and was he himself an honorary disciple of that old bloody order as some have suggested when he was a seminarian? That old communist serial killer knew a thing or two about making people disappear when he needed to, and he probably could have given the Jesuits a lesson or two in that department, or maybe it was the other way around, who knows?

In researching and commencing this book, I am naturally aware that we are now entering deep into enemy territory, and in turning up those previous rocks of history to try and see what may lie underneath concerning these clerics and their previous religious methods as they try to achieve naked power at any cost in this fallen world. This can be very dangerous for the researcher. I also somehow see their clerical hands behind the Roswell incident of 1947 that focused so much useless attention towards extraterrestrial arrivals from another galaxy, and foolishly ignoring the saving grace of the Saviour Jesus Christ.

The Great Fire of London in 1666 was another example of their possible involvement, with the Jews naturally blamed for this tragedy.

I therefore I have to suggest the power of Satan (it's his world after all, and I also do not believe that one man - i.e., the pope - can control the thinking and lives of nearly two billion people, it's just impossible). So, there has to be an inner Vatican group that promotes and has always pursued that church's future political financial and spiritual agenda. According to the author Leo Lyon Zagami: "The spirit of Satan along with his gang of paedophiles, Satanists, Mafiosi and Masonic businessmen are leading the church of Rome into an inexorable decline." Well, he said it, not me, and it also has to be remembered that Catholicism is not Biblical Christianity by any means, but a fabricated and conniving pagan religion founded in the 4th century by Constantine and perfected by Augustine in the 5th century.

Just look at the symbols of that pagan Roman dynasty, i.e., the bishop's mitre. It is the symbol of Dagon, the old Roman fish god. Excuse the pun, but very fishy, I suggest, and there are many more of these demonic/pagan symbols that the church of Rome is stacked to the brim with. So, if you're still a supplicant practicing that religion, then listen to the Book of Revelation and its warning: "Come out of her my people."

It has been reported of the Jesuits that: "If you don't love them you must fear them," or, "They are a public plague and a plague of the world." Wow! Is this the mafia we are discussing here? No, it's the Jesuits, and here a few more to add to this tale of danger and deception that resides in our fallen world.

From Abraham Lincoln: "This [civil] war (1860-1865) would never have been possible without the sinister influence of the Jesuits." I further suggest that they organised the murder of Lincoln as well. His own personal connection with the Jesuits comes from the time when he personally defended Charles Chiniquy (then a Catholic priest) on a trumped-up rape charge, and other convenient felonies brought in against him by the Catholic Church. Lincoln also called to the stand a bishop Foley, and after an erratic trial his client was found not guilty, then apparently later on the way out of the courthouse Lincoln witnessed his client Charles Chiniquy standing alone and in tears, and asked why? Chiniquy turned to him thanking him for he had all he done to maintain his innocence and the kindness he had shown the former priest in assisting him in clearing his besmirched name but then fortuitously warned the future president that the Jesuits had very long memories and they would somehow where possible seek their revenge for how he had challenged them and belittled them in the courthouse. The priest would leave the church of Rome and, it seems, take most of his parish with him, wonderful!

As Lloyd Lewis writes in his book: "Chiniquy developed a lasting admiration for the tall lawyer and travelled to the White House at least three times to warn Lincoln against murderous plots which he imagined the Jesuits were forming against the President."

The same author also quotes another story that cannot be confirmed:

"The suspicious deaths also of Washington, Jefferson, Monroe, Harrison, Garfield, and Zachary Taylor do seem to point towards foul play in how these prominent men, no friends of the Jesuits, met their suspicious deaths" (I do hope they were saved). I could name many other 20th century politicians as well as past presidents caught in the cross fire of revenge killings.

It is further claimed that Lincoln shortly before his death had been asked by an Illinois clergyman the question: "Do you love Jesus?" Lincoln had replied: "When I left Springfield, I asked the people to pray for me. I was not a Christian. When I buried my son Willie, the severest day of my life, I was not a Christian. But when I went to Gettysburg and saw the graves of thousands of our soldiers, I then and there consecrated myself to Christ. Yes, I do love Jesus."

We should all take note, of course, that our lives are like a vapour, here today and gone tomorrow. Always be ready therefore to meet the Lord if you are saved, for all will have to give an account at the Judgment Seat for every thought, word and deed one day.

President Lincoln was shot on the 14th April 1865, dying a day later, being Good Friday in fact. The same day, curiously enough, that the ill-fated Titanic went down in the Atlantic Sea, being 15th April 1912.

As regards the Titanic, strangely enough, an invited young Jesuit priest named Francis Browne was on board the liner, and apparently took many photographs with a camera given to him by his uncle, the then bishop of Cloyne in Ireland. Browne seems to have been given free access to photograph where and who he wanted (maybe by Captain Smith, perhaps a Jesuit agent provocateur or a coadjutor himself?) The young priest later reluctantly disembarked with strict orders from his superior by a sent telegram that ordered him to: "Get off the ship, Provincial." It seems he had been previously invited by a first-class travelling family to proceed with them to New York as their guest, then after asking permission from his superior this suspicious telegram arrived. He quickly disembarked at Queenstown. All very strange and suspicious I suggest for the life of this 'lucky' priest, as one famous actor remarked. He lived to tell the story; sadly, over a thousand did not. I will be looking later at the serious ramifications of the sinking of this great ship and the murders of those who died, 1,517 I believe, but there may have been many more on board, such as stowaways, and some still unaccounted for.

But back to Abraham Lincoln's assassination, prepared it seems on the orders of the Jesuit black pope to punish him for his prominent role in the Chiniquy trial, and his further questioning of the Roman clergy in the court house. Always remember the Jesuits have been cursed with having long memories it seems (I've also heard that the IRA also suffer from this revenge gene) frequently used against those who deny or attempt to unmask them as they lurk in the dark cloisters of the Vatican corridors, for as the Holy Bible warns: "Men loved darkness rather than light, because their deeds were evil." But of course everything is possible until proven otherwise, and that is an aspect of Loyola's Jesuit cult.

Other quotes worth mentioning about this unscriptural priestly tribe come from Napoleon Bonaparte, who said: "The aim of this military order [the Jesuits] is power. Wherever the Jesuits are admitted they will be masters."

Jesuit theologian, Michele Schmaus, arrogantly wrote: "The national socialist [Nazi] commandments and those of the Catholic Church have the same aim." And listen in amazement to what the German Jesuit superior general Franz Wernz said: "The church can condemn heretics to death, for any rights they have are only through our tolerance and these rights are apparent, not real."

These sound like little clerical tin gods issuing threats and orders, and they will surely burn in the eternal fires of hell for these sickening unrepentant remarks issued against so many.

We should be always thankful to our glorious and gracious God that we have been given the Holy Bible as our peaceful weapon against them, the true word of God, and of course the free and saving gift of everlasting life through the LORD Jesus Christ. For these past Jesuits, there will be nothing but damnation in the outer darkness of hell awaiting them. But we are commanded today to pray for these powerful men, however difficult that might well be for us.

And what about this little gem from Hitler himself, said with some pride in his maniacal voice: "I have learnt most of all from the Jesuit order. I will tell you a secret. I am founding an order (the S.S.) and in Himmler, I see our own Ignatius Loyola."

He later added, with menace: "As for the Jews, I am just carrying on with the same policy which the Catholic church has adopted for fifteen hundred years, when it has regarded the Jews as dangerous and pushed them into ghettoes, etc."

Those ghettoes he talked about would later morph into working concentration death camps with many being staffed by Roman Catholics in all branches of administration, and with the support and knowledge of the local diocesan bishops, many who outdid themselves to be more Nazi-like than the Nazis themselves.

No shame from such apostate 'men of God'

Pope Clement XIII did suppress the Jesuit order (a brave man indeed!) and remarked afterwards to a worried cardinal that: "This will be my death," and the old boy was correct; they poisoned him. He would sadly say on his deathbed: "Alas, I knew they would poison me but I did not expect to die so slowly," and he did, probably unsaved, and certainly never deferential to them.

Pope Pius V was murdered for the simple reason that he objected to the Jesuits using the holy name of Jesus, a bad move on his part.

In 1813 Jesuit "general" Brzozowski was somehow able to negotiate the release of pope Pius VII, and he incidentally would have had the honour of crowning Napoleon emperor, but as we know, Bonaparte did that honour himself instead. From strict captivity interment, this pope had been placed there by Napoleon. Later the pope would reinstate the order back into the ecclesiastical fold and he would forever be in their debt. He would arrogantly threaten any who might criticise the order.

I also suggest the Jesuits were involved with the implementation of many Masonic lodges and worked in collusion with top mafia families and maybe the Illuminati itself. The late Malachi Martin himself, a former Jesuit, surprisingly suggested this some years ago. Some today even suggest Martin was murdered in suspicious circumstances in 1999, well, who knows?

We should remember that today there are over 83 world regions of Jesuit influence, with 10 being located in the USA alone.

Concerning the still unsolved suspicious death of pope John Paul I in 1978 (the '33-day' pope) he had foolishly and naïvely spoken out in calling for left-wing priests promoting communism/Marxism to be disciplined by their bishops as well as ordering an overdue overhaul of the secretive Vatican bank and questioning his church's "cosy" relationship with the Marxists in Moscow.

The Jesuits would not and could not allow or accept any of these implementations to happen. I also suggest a successful idea of obtaining the paid services of a professional actor (union rates, I hope) to portray and remove the vacillating pope Paul VI for whatever reasons, probably because he would not allow his beloved church to swallow the poison cup of Marxist/Jesuit liberation theology that was slowly being diluted into his church's calendar in the 1960s, courtesy of Vatican II of course.

If you're not sure about this theory, just look at some of the photographs taken of him before and after Vatican II.

So, was he murdered after all, or wounded, or maybe imprisoned, or quietly drugged up then left lingering in some secluded Swiss monastery, forgotten and alone? There had been an assassination attempt on Paul on his life in Manila in 1970, and he may have been wounded in this attack.

Also, an attempt on pope John Paul II in Rome has never been entirely explained, he after all had placed his own designated choice to run the order after Jesuit superior "general" Pedro Arrupe suffered a stroke in 1981, and this certainly cooled relations between the Jesuits and the Polish pope. And what about the assassination attempts in 2007 and 2008 by a "mad" woman directed against Benedict XVI? All very strange, and was she perhaps a "Manchurian candidate" acting under orders, but from whom? And what about the remarks by cardinal Romeo on a flight to China some years ago, claiming that Benedict "could be the victim of an assassination plot" later that year? Did this cardinal from Palermo (not a Jesuit) know something we don't? And why do I see the sinister manicured hands of Loyola's troops somewhere in these woods of doubt and disorder?!?

I also wonder why they have waited so long to put their own man in the top job on the so-called "throne of Peter." Rubbish of course! Peter never resided in Rome, and he certainly did not expire there.

Why did Lenin suspiciously in 1922 reinstate that accursed proscribed religious order back into the fledgling Soviet Union society after Tsar Alexander had expelled them in 1820? And did not Marx famously claim that: "Religion is the opium of the people"? Well, obviously not the Jesuits who later quickly built a Russian college in 1929 in Moscow to perhaps assist Lenin in bringing in the brutal murder and almost extinction of Russian orthodox church members and hierarchy. And what about the terrible gulag concentration camps that would swallow up millions into their gulags dotted across godless

Russia? All with the aid of his secret murderous police, a body of bloodthirsty thugs, no less.

And where were the Jesuits in the genocide of the Armenians in 1915? Almost 2 million innocent people were part of "the final solution" genocide initiated by a Muslim Turkish government, and of course, the Greek Orthodox Church was almost decimated in the final sweep later. Was this a religious crusade against that church, because within years both the Russian and Greek orthodox faiths were almost destroyed along with most of the people who worshipped in that religion? And of course under the Nazis' anti-Semitic "final solution" Hitler, Himmler and Heydrich (all Roman Catholics, one must note) were eagerly instrumental themselves with the might of the Third Reich in the organised murder of millions of Jews. But the church of Rome continues and flourishes, does it not? This was and always had been on the Jesuits' wicked agenda prepared at the Council of Trent in 1545-1563 to quickly extinguish all other churches, specifically born-again Bible believers who have not and will not submit to the apostate boot of the church of Rome!

And there are many more examples I could choose, of course, but it is worth examining the Jesuits' promotion of Hitler and their very cosy connection with him. In Germany in the 1930s for example in his ascendancy to power whilst imprisoned in Lansberg prison not far from Munich. In 1923-1924 he began dictating his memoirs (if you can call them that) to his cellmate Rudolph Hess, later to be published as Mein Kampf.

Into this diabolical and depraved plot enters an ambitious Jesuit priest named Bernhard Stempfle, who each day, it seems, cycled to the prison and collected Hess' neatly typed pages of Hitler's tripe of anti-Semitic thoughts, the memories of his youth and his future plans for the Jewish race. The Jesuit priest then happily edited them and prepared them for the Nazi's own printer, but more importantly, he was also a member of Hitler's personal inner circle. I believe he was also feeding important information back to Rome to the then superior "general" Ledochowski (more on him later).

He may well have originally become acquainted with Hitler and Hess and maybe Himmler through the dubious secret societies that were so much a staple diet of the political esoteric menus then thriving in post-war Germany. For example, the Vril group, the Black Sun society and the Thule group, all very much into the worship and study of mysticism and dangerous occult practices, and probably no doubt connected and controlled by the Jesuit hierarchy themselves.

The Jesuits had infiltrated these mystical movements, probably because of their bizarre beliefs and promotion of the existence of extraterrestrials coming from space and the Vatican's belief in the hollow earth theory.

In fact, the alien belief is very much on the Jesuit religious agenda today under this present Jesuit pope. However, Jesuit priest Stempfle seems to have gotten dangerously close to Hitler's ill-fated niece, Geli Raubal. Too close, I would suggest. He would be later murdered in 1934 as a victim of the infamous "night of the long knives."

The Jesuits of the 21st century have skillfully created their own (not of the Holy Bible, of course) personal "Jesus." The false Messiah of their devious creation is a crude depiction of a grinning Cuban cigar-smoking Che Guevara armed with a loaded Kalashnikov rifle, of course, and always on the side of the striking proletariat. Remember: "Workers of the world unite. You have nothing to lose but your chains," wrote Marx in 1848 and probably assisted by a Jesuit from Farm Street, London (see 2 Corinthians 11:1-4).

Marx was never a worker of course, nor did he ever do an honest day's work in his life, but shamefully sponged off Engels whenever he could. The working creed of the Jesuits has always been that the end justifies the means if it brings or promotes the greater good and their understanding of their personal god.

Just remember the terrible price paid by millions who would not bow down to the pope or his evil authority.

The creeping globalisation of the Jesuits continues today with the obliging press as well as the Internet and naturally Hollywood acting in compliance with the daily dictates that arrive from Rome. An unhealthy abundance of popular films, such as ET, Close Encounters, Independence Day, Signs *and* Contact, frequently invade our cinemas and now our television screens, seemingly influencing us to joyfully await and welcome a "friendly" alien invasion, with this pope naturally acting as a proposed mediator to the new world government.

He is even prepared, it seems, to welcome and baptize them when that mothership slowly descends to (where else?) St.

Peter's Square in Rome, and naturally, CNN, ABC, Fox News and NBC have been altered to this "Breaking News Alert." All will watch and many will welcome these demons of Satan now at last showing themselves. They will happily pose as our friends but they are really demons and enemies of mankind.

Well, that's the current Jesuit scenario being quietly promoted (if that's the word) to an unaware population. Yet the born-again Bible believer knows they will return with the Lord one day after the much awaited and anticipated pre-tribulation rapture. Amen!

There's a popular theory circulating today promoted by so many misguided academics concerning the so-called and rather silly "big bang" theory, which was conventionally invented and introduced to the scientific world by a certain George Lemaitre, a Belgium Jesuit priest no less and a buddy of Albert Einstein, which seems to me to suggest that they hoped this might give him some street credibility in the murky world of evolution. Out of this uncertain nether of the false "big bang" many other civilisations were created it seems in our own universe and maybe beyond, then some time in the future, maybe sooner, these coming *allies* or *visitors* from other galaxies will descend onto a defenceless earth to pay homage to the Roman pontiff, and of course they will be baptized by him as well as being initiated into other useless Roman practices.

Listen and learn if you will of their efficient network of spies and paid agents and what they have achieved, for example. This is what the 18th Jesuit secretary general Michelangelo Tamburini (1706-1730) boasted to a visitor, perhaps the Duke de Brissac, when he said: "See, Sir, from this chamber, I govern not only Paris but to China, not only to China but to the world without anyone knowing how I do it."

But whom does this dangerous or deceived boaster sound like to you? Don't we read of another dark and powerful person, who made a similar and sinister statement many years ago to the Son of God: "And the devil, taking him up into an high mountain, shewed unto him all the kingdoms of the world in a moment of time. And the devil said unto him, All this power will I give thee, and the glory of them: for that is delivered unto me; and to whomsoever, I will I give it. If thou therefore wilt worship me, all shall be thine. And Jesus answered and said unto him, Get thee behind me, Satan: for it is written, Thou shalt worship the Lord thy God, and him only shalt thou serve" (Luke 4:5-8).

One would do well to bold the last part of this and take great heed to it: "And Jesus answered and said unto him, Get thee behind me, Satan: for it is written, Thou shalt worship the Lord thy God, and him only shalt thou serve."

One must worship Almighty God and not man, whether he is a Jesuit priest, a TV celebrity, or politician, or a pop star!

I would not have expected however such a statement from the mouth of a so-called "holy man," but from the mouth of the head of the CIA, or the Russian FSB (the former KGB) to boast about at any "boozy" embassy garden barbecue. But more importantly, if that Jesuit general had that power, then what can they use now against King James Bible-believers!

Wow, I hate to think. But always remember, we are protected by the full armour of the Lord. Amen.

Well in advance, the Jesuits have prepared the secret church blueprints for influencing this world. All they have to do is take them out from their trusted "chubb primus" safes located somewhere in Vatican City to use in ushering in their inflicted new world order to be perpetrated against a sleeping uncertain frightened world that needs Jesus Christ now more than ever.

The Jesuits can offer nothing but doubt and deception, but Jesus Christ offers the gift of eternal life to forever reside with Him in heaven. "And ye shall know the truth, and the truth shall make you free" (John 8:32).

But always know your enemy and that wickedness in high places. For the apostle Paul would tell us such: "For we wrestle not against flesh and blood, but against principalities, against powers, against the rulers of the darkness of this world, against spiritual wickedness in high places" (Ephesians 6:12).

The Jesuit symbol

During my research for this book, I noted that during one Jesuit superior's watch, six popes were murdered by means of poison, and suspicion has long been pointed at their ecclesiastical door. With a Jesuit pope – the first in fact – we cannot rule out a future Jesuit-controlled American president installed in Washington, maybe by this time next year. These previous Vatican assassins have brought nothing but pain and death through history to all who try to obstruct them and will continue to do so. Their quest for a so-called "holy Roman empire" is endless with their man the pope calling the "shots." We at this ministry will remain vigilant and always watchful until the Lord calls all Bible believers out from this fallen world, into the coming joyful rapture.

Chapter 2: "The Curse Of Jekyll Island"

Barren-looking marshland at Jekyll Island

The unexplained performance of young Francis Browne aboard the RMS Titanic's maiden voyage is very perplexing and will probably never be explained. But I suggest that he was doing much more than snapping black-and-white Kodak pictures. Remember their advertising slogan "You press the button, we do the rest" of smiling, posed privileged passengers on the sunny upper decks of the ship? Had he perhaps been entrusted instead by his Jesuit superior to deliver an important sealed envelope to Captain Edward John Smith? Himself perhaps a Jesuit temporal coadjutor? (He was also called the millionaires' captain, it seems.) Regardless of the purpose, that lost letter - like the captain's body - would never be recovered.

There are still so many unanswered questions about the Titanic calamity. Was the captain inebriated? Or did a submarine torpedo the ship for insurance purposes, certainly benefiting the overflowing cash coffers of JP Morgan afterwards when he put in an insurance claim. Was there perhaps a suspicious steering blunder from the bridge? Or perhaps more startlingly, was it not the Titanic but the RMS Olympic ship that sunk in the dark that cold night? Or was it the curse of the pharaohs that doomed this ship to destruction and death because - it is claimed - there was a bound mummy of a young Egyptian temple priestess on board for the voyage, sealed in a sarcophagus no less? Of course, this should have been stored in the cargo hold (company regulations) but was instead located very near the bridge of the ship. What was all this about and on whose orders was it placed in this location and why? Some even whispered the ship was cursed. Well, maybe! They did very foolishly say how even "God couldn't sink it."

Yet this popular captain had over 24 seagoing years of experience on the high seas (but had perhaps failed his mariner's licence before this voyage for some reason, it has been suggested). Yet he seems to have had some sort of mental mishap of mismanagement, as later remembered by his crew at the inquest. Others on the sinking ship recalled that some claimed he also seemed vague before that fatal "night to remember."

However, what is of historical interest to me is that amongst the many affluent passengers who treated themselves on that doomed maiden voyage yet tragically did not survive the harsh Atlantic Sea were three of the wealthiest men in the world at that time, namely, Benjamin Guggenheim, Isidor Strauss, and Jacob John Astor. In fact, their total financial worth today would be a staggering eleven billion dollars, can you believe?

It's important also to remember historically that since their inception in 1540 and for hundreds of years afterwards, the Jesuits have been forcibly expelled from a hundred countries for plotting, interfering and causing strife in government affairs of state. In fact, there may have been more nations because many of those countries no longer exist today.

Not only were the Jesuits being expelled from countries that they were "spiritually occupying" you could say, but all their goods (i.e., finances, jewels, gold, and pearls) would have, of course, been confiscated by hostile governments in the process. This obviously denied them massive profits from, amongst other things, the lucrative opium and silk trading routes then stretching from Japan to Madagascar, to La Paz, Bolivia, to Zakawei and even to Shanghai. And would not some of these countries' naval fleets deny the Jesuits the use of the lucrative shipping sea lanes to transport their cargos? I'm sure they would, without doubt! (See Revelation 18:9-20.)

And what about the shocking cost and degradation of taking human life in the equation? These have been described by O.C. Lambert in his book *Catholicism Against Itself?* on page 217 where he describes frequent Jesuit agitation and anger directed amongst peoples in America, especially New Mexico, where indigenous people were whipped, starved, and brutalised by named Jesuit priests, then forcibly converted to Catholicism by the gun or other sordid means if necessary. This is described on page 239.

Mr. Lambert also records that later these poor defenceless people "were compelled to work and were beaten at the will of the 'Padre'." Umm, now this seems like some good old Jesuit charm being administered by Loyola's "men in black." And of course, these are not isolated cases he records, but probably occurring in many other parts of the world.

So, it stands to reason - I propose - that the besieged Jesuit order certainly required and also needed very quickly (for obvious reasons and for financial need) to acquire their own private bank or clearinghouse and to then fruitfully expand wherever possible - even more so as the new century dawned -. And where better, I suggest, than to look toward the horizons of the so-called New World (the Americas, of course).

"Money makes the world go round," proclaimed a popular song of yesterday. Scripture would also tell us how the "love of money is the root of all evil" (1 Timothy 6:10). But it seems that the continuing haemorrhaging of Jesuit cash almost brought the "Society of Jesus" to its cassocked knees. However, first some important history: in 1777, the Illuminati entered the world political stage in Bavaria, a Catholic/Jesuit stronghold, with the compliant support of Fredrick the Great and Catherine of Russia.

Interestingly enough, when Jesuit missionary Matteo Ricci journeyed to China in 1582, he easily complied with the local native custom of donning silk robes and platting his hair. It seems he saw nothing wrong - much to the dismay of the local Dominican clergy - with local Chinese parishioners in his church inserting Confucius' intercessions into their Catholic prayers and referring to their "god" as "Lord of heaven."

Well, well. It seems these missionary Jesuits were totally committed to ecumenism even then. And it seems the same religious running order of service was being performed by the Jesuits in India with the use of inserting native Hindu gods into the Catholic liturgy. In other words, be all things to all men. Or: the ends justify the means.

Listen to this from author Alan Woodrow, who claims that: "China never fully accepted the Catholic church. In 1982, the communist Beijing government refused to take part in the Catholic celebrations organised in Rome, to celebrate the 400th anniversary of Matteo Ricci's' arrival in Macao."

As regards the Jesuits' unhealthy relationship with Freemasonry, the late author W. L. Wilmshurst, a Mason himself and a noted historian, writes in his informative book The Meaning of Masonry: "The early Catholic Church involved a sequence of three initiatory rites identical in intention with those of the craft (masonry). The names given to those who had qualified in these rites respectively were Catechumens, Leitutrgoi, and Priests or Presbyters; which in turn are identifiable with our own Entered Apprentices, Fellow Crafts and Master Masons."

Interesting to know and don't forget dear reader, the terrible blood oaths they utter during clerical services by all Jesuit novices, much of this deriving from masonry and witchcraft.

So there you have it: out of the Catholic church was conceived freemasonry, and with the church of Constantine in 312 AD borrowing so much then in worship and vestments from pagan Babylon, to later be seen in the evolving church of Rome, with much as it is today.

The still secretive working relationship between the Jesuits and the house of Rothschild remains very much hidden today, and they both seem to have survived the ups and downs of politics and frequent financial money market cash crises that blighted so much of the 20th century. Yet what is soon to arrive as written in the book of Revelation (under the mark of the beast) is simply "comply or die" and a sharpened guillotine being brought out of mothballs, oiled and prepared, to be used again as it was once used long ago to perfection in the Place de la Revolution during the French reign of terror in 1790 (Jesuit orchestrated perhaps).

Incidentally, this Parisian location would later be known as Palace de la Concorde where that Masonic Egyptian obelisk with its occult hieroglyphics takes pride of place. No two ways about it, the guillotine will beckon to those who refuse to accept the mark to sell or trade, and they will be forcibly detained without trial in prepared internment camps.

It is the prepared financial mark of the beast or a barcode that all citizens will be forced to accept and display. And remember:

there will be no choice in what was prophesied the book of Revelation two thousand years ago and is still yet to come.

The banking matrix system as we know today has travelled very far since old Meyer Rothschild opened his first counting house in Germany, acquiring even more wealth and power, much of it still operating today.

The disgraced financier Robert Maxwell once claimed that: "If you owe the bank enough, you own the bank." Well, he should know because he nearly demolished many of the City of London's banks with his sad squandering and thieving of other people's pensions and savings in the early 1990s.

The City of London interestingly is also a city within a city, rather like the Vatican in Rome. I do perhaps wonder if they have reciprocal arrangements with each other, and there certainly must be a resilient Jesuit influence in these London financial fiefdoms that will always benefit Rome. Oh, and do you remember the BICC crash in 1991? Well, one comedian later called it, "The Bank of Crooks and Criminals International." What happened, I ask, to all those missing millions of dollars never to be seen again?

So, I suggest the Jesuits would be quite at home in this habitat of greed and gold. Of course, all deception and deceit from organised religion and their cohorts in the NWO will continue until the welcomed Rapture comes and mercifully and joyfully removes the born-again Bible-believer out of this failed corrupt wicked world to be with the Lord Jesus Christ forever. There, we will gain joy and jubilation in our new spiritual home furnished and prepared for our habitation and delight, and with not a Jesuit in sight. Praise the Lord!

Now, with the previous murders of so many on the Titanic in 1912 written about earlier, we should remember that the dead included those powerful bankers. It seems these three had opposed the creation of the Federal Reserve Bank (FRB) for whatever grounds but were now out of the way. Hence, its conception and creation could go ahead unhindered. One month later after secret discussions on Jekyll Island and with a hand-picked consortium of prominent bankers brought in by motorboat, they could, at last, get down to business in creating the FRB in total secrecy. Don't men always love darkness where the truth is concerned?

The Federal Reserve Bank finally saw the light of day, and also included in that package of misery was the introduction of a compulsory income tax (IRS).

A footnote of interest is that World War I began in August 1914. Was this all pre-arranged? Jekyll Island in Georgia is of interest to me and I should first mention here that I have never visited that island. However, some years ago, I did read a holiday survey in a dentists' waiting room, if I recall, that had been compiled from tourists who had stayed in that location. According to their lasting impressions: they had found it depressing and invasive, or as one said "very creepy."

I suppose Jekyll Island was rather akin in those pre-war halcyon days to the rich gentlemen of the elite East Coast establishment who visited it to sample and enjoy the Island's hospitality, legal or illegal, similar to that infamous and well-known Bohemian Grove estate much sought after by West Coast philanders (both venues being popular and secluded private playgrounds for rich pampered men such as the Morgans, Rothschilds, Rockefellers, and other favoured politicians of the lodge and church prelates). Many of these men had attended Yale University themselves and been initiated into the notorious and Satanic "skull and bones" fraternity, it seems.

More importantly, it was a secluded location where these men could indulge in their own perverted sexual tastes in private as well as pursue and recite the oaths and rituals of their secret societies, as seen so often at the Bohemian Grove "celebrations" today. Which brings me back to the Jesuits.

Interestingly, Leo Zagami writes in his book *Pope Francis, the Last Pope* that: "The Jesuits are not only a Catholic order but a secret society dedicated to magic and deception." He also quotes Jean Charles Pichon, who wrote in his book that: "One point is certain: the Jesuits have always given great attention to magic."

Later on Jekyll Island (six men and perhaps more, and Jesuits well versed in the complexities of financial matters) would journey secretly to this island. The men would use only their first names (for security, it is said) and this chosen island would later be described as: "The richest, the most exclusive, the most inaccessible club in the world." There, after precise plotting and planning, the fledgeling Federal Reserve Bank first witnessed the light of a new dawn, but a dark night for the free world, all courtesy of these men and the Illuminati.

Yet does not Luke 12:2 remind us: "For there is nothing covered that shall not be revealed; neither hid that shall not be known." Judgment will come one day to those purveyors of the black arts.

In retrospect, I suggest perhaps the new official title being printed on the new currency then should have read the "Federal Reserve Jekyll Bank" but perhaps that's too obvious for the prestigious Wall Street Journal to print or promote.

I do seriously propose, however, that a senior Jesuit (in mufti of course, and upon personal written instructions from the 25th Superior General Franz Wernz) arrived at the island's gated harbour from one of the ten Jesuit American provinces, having being invited to attend the meeting and bringing a financial working agenda in his briefcase already drawn up by his superiors for the assembled waiting group to approve or disapprove. I find it no coincidence either that from 1566-1736 the Jesuits had actually owned Jekyll Island (can you believe?) after previously taking it or stealing it from a group of Huguenots. I'm not sure why they were there or what their story was.

Formerly, it had been the habitat of Native Indians. At the time of the proposed meeting on the island, it was then owned by JP Morgan, who seemed in those days to be everywhere, always planning and always plotting. A man whose influence is still very much alive today on Wall Street.

Either way, ten months after the sinking of the doomed Titanic, the Jesuits were now financially secure. A deal of sorts had been reached. They now owned or were an important partner in the banking system, now along with the Rothschilds, Chase Manhattan bank in New York, and with Lazard Bros and Goldman Sachs, both still happily operating today in the turbulent financial markets of the world.

The official proposed financial bill was passed in Congress in 1913 and signed by President Woodrow Wilson. I'm not really sure if he was a practising Mason or simply a fair-weather friend, as they say, to the lodge. Certainly, his right-hand man "Colonel" Edwin House wore many hats in his career, maybe even an Illuminati beret, and he seems to fit the bill as an important group "points man."

But for the Jesuits, the Bank of America would later be added to that growing portfolio of blue-chip investments. I suggest they were now finally secure, never again to be expelled or humiliated or to witness their finances depleted or distributed to someone else.

Incidentally, on the important education front, something which should never be ignored, the Order can boast of administrating over 30 universities functioning today in the U.S. alone. I am sure they always found it possible to take or grasp any advantages, and to appropriate whatever rights they could acquire to further the aims and ambitions of the Order.

This chosen island they once owned offered them easy access to possible land on the secluded East Coast with the Carolinas, Massachusetts, and Maine states in their religious sights. The fundamental Biblical belief of the settled inhabitants was practised by many in their thriving communities, with the open use of the Geneva and King James Bibles, the two books the Jesuits despised and had resolved to destroy after the infamous and heretical Council of Trent. It would have then been feasible and possible to quickly invade these locations with paid mercenaries and agent provocateurs and a small-armed force to be silently landed at night on lonely deserted darkened beaches on that seaboard for a military-style invasion to secure and bring the eastern seaboard under Rome's Catholic control. It didn't happen, of course, but I'm sure detailed invasion plans were drawn up and large sums of monies were set aside by the Jesuits to invade from land and by sea if possible. Yet, as usual, God had other plans for the protection of His people in America, ever loyal to Him and never to pagan Rome.

It's worth considering the mental state of Loyola's personality at this point. All published accounts claim details of his flesh wounds sustained in battles, especially on his leg, and the painful discomfort he must have endured. And there is no doubt about this, but I do have to speculate: was there some initial brain damage inflicted upon him early in his career as a serving soldier? Perhaps by a musket butt or a stray leaden ball that altered his future outlook on life? So often, a serious head injury can and does cause a permanent personality change to the patient. Many times that damaged area of the skull seems to be located in the cerebral cortex affecting the limbic system, it seems. Loyola would also have deranged and dangerous conversations with a serpent in a cave, which not only sounds somewhat occultist but very worryingly could reflect a disturbed and receptive mindset!

Some years ago I made the acquaintance of a pastor in our town, and he had a very pronounced extrovert personality, as I recall. I found it very grating and he always demanded attention about whatever he was doing both in and outside his church, and I suspect he also enjoyed immense flattery when offered (a very vain man). Strangely enough, around at the same time, I met another man who had known him when they were both teenagers and just out of school. They were good friends, and I was informed by this man that his friend, the future pastor, had suffered a serious accident on a motorbike to his head. Now I'm not sure of the details, but it certainly changed his personality, this ex-friend had told me, most specifically that he had somehow "gotten into religion in a big way." He had never shown any interest before in religious classes at school.

This same form of accidental mishap also occurred to some other prominent historical religious leaders of the past, for example, Ellen White (Seventh-day Adventist) and John Nelson Darby (Brethren assembly), and the late controversial Lord Longford. They had all suffered injuries to the skull.

Perhaps if Loyola had not sustained a possible head wound in war or elsewhere we might have been spared much of the terrible Inquisition and the subsequent birth of the Jesuits, and the young Loyola might have instead found and enjoyed a career as a matador or a strolling dashing Gaucho serenading those Spanish señoritas with his flamenco guitar, and naturally astride a strolling palomino horse.

Interestingly, government-commissioned research of notorious serial killers of the 20th century seems to point to the important medical fact that many of them had also suffered accidental head traumas in their youth that affected their future moods and morals, but not the sadistic methods they used, it seems, in the terrible suffering they systematically inflicted upon their innocent victims (mainly young women). Fortunately, they were detained by the police, later being incarcerated or executed before they could subject their victims to even more dreadful deaths. But it doesn't have to be all negative, of course.

For instance, just examine the career change of the famous French impressionist painter Paul Gauguin who for some reason (maybe an accident) deserted his employment as a stockbroker in Paris at the Bourse, leaving his family, later sailing to the Polynesian Islands, there to paint and lead a debauched life. That certainly was a life-changing decision on his part of which I suggest the art world today has been eternally gratefully and financially secure ever since. I've also read of some people who after suffering an accidental head trauma were quickly able to speak and converse in many foreign languages. (One, of course, cannot rule out demonic influence in such cases.)

Others have been able to master a difficult musical instrument, almost playing professionally without ever enjoying a musical lesson in their life, and one woman could remember herself playing viola in the royal court orchestra of the king of Prussia no less, and amazingly remembered Mozart conducting the orchestra briskly as she played for him. It seems she had fallen down the stairs backwards. How awful. Apparently, this is quite common today, so be careful. There is so much of the personality traits that are locked in our bodies that we do not understand, or perhaps we are not meant to.

It is worth now considering the dangerous alliance between the Masonic lodges then and the Catholic church, or rather an unholy alliance, I should say, that both have used each other's skills and methods.

Loyola had previously changed his name from Iñigo to Ignatius (was this before or after his accident, I wonder), and he may have been involved with one of the numerous secret societies then so prevalent in Spain, one such being Los Alumbrados. This group encouraged and practised a form of Gnosticism as well as other secret rituals, these being practised even today in numerous Masonic lodges in many countries. Of course, many of these rituals and mock sacrifices and blood-curdling oaths evolved from the murky Babylonian temples, supervised by the pagan priests and priestesses of the numerous temples that thrived then. Now with a few friends gathered around the young Loyola, one being Francis Borgia, a co-founder of the Jesuits, it seems they would later call themselves for some reason "the grey habits." This would later bring them naturally to the notice of the police spies.

Loyola would also be arrested by the militia of the dreaded Inquisition in 1527, for some crime brought against him, perhaps due to a religious heresy, it has been suggested. A written report circulating at the time described him as: "Treacherous, brutal, vindictive." Later, he would be released from confinement for some reason. Now this I find very unusual in the circumstances because the interrogators in those days weren't in the business of offering instant unconditional freedom to a held prisoner unless that person could be of an important use to them in the future as a spy or rather to be used like a "sleeper" still very much used today by most, if not all, intelligence services in the world.

In 1528 Loyola would arrive in Paris. Later in 1530, he would journey to London. For whatever purpose is unclear to me, but maybe it was to attempt to murder the brave and brilliant William Tyndale in his print shop, the man who had translated the Holy Bible into English? Or perhaps to be involved with some Catholics in assisting the disgraced Cardinal Wolsey to escape to Europe? Wolsey died of natural causes anyway. Or was it simply to raise money from prominent protected Catholic families? Or maybe it was an espionage mission of some other importance entrusted to him by the Dominican police in Spain? Or perhaps he was just acting as a simple courier and had perhaps acquired a peculiar taste for that "cloak-and-dagger way of life" by then. If so, this would certainly keep him (and all those future Jesuit spies that followed him in the Order) in good stead.

And don't forget Himmler's sadistic S.S. troops, who would be deeply influenced by that Jesuit military order of precision and prayer, and its mandatory strict code of loyalty to Hitler, and to a lesser extent, Himmler himself.

He [Himmler] "possessed the largest library on the Jesuit order and had studied it for years," wrote Walter Schellenberg, a close confidant of Himmler, and in their basic training, all raw recruits would have been presented a copy of the Jesuit spiritual exercises, or *Exercitia Spiritualia* given to them to be carried at all time in their rucksacks and studied whenever on military manoeuvres.

The S.S. would flourish for 13 more terrible years in Europe until the defeat of the Nazi war machine in 1945. Then thousands of fleeing Nazi war criminals with newly prepared Red Cross passports, courtesy of the Vatican, would seek a new life in Catholic South America and beyond. But the Jesuit order disregarded nothing in those dangerous post-war years, having learnt a great deal. Instead, they turned their attention to surviving the so-called "cold war era" under their newly elected superior general, a 57 year old Belgian named, John Baptist Janssen.

The French historian Pierre Dominique correctly recorded that: "The Jesuits have their secret abode in the Vatican...From there they survey the universal church with the cold, calculating eye of the politician." But even then, those doctors of deception would be kept active until 1991 when the cold war expired, simply and easily and without a shot being fired (rather like a whimper or a passing breeze). Probably as God had planned it all to happen anyway.

Remember: "Whatsoever is born of God overcometh the world" (1 John 5:4).

To be continued...

Chapter 3: "Enter The Count"

Jesuit superior general count Halke Von Ledochowski

As regards the Jesuits and their founding, after numerous false starts and some disruptions, the Society of Jesus was finally constituted on Assumption Day in 1534 at the chapel of Notre Dame de Montmartre. Now the designed Jesuit network of bribery, assassinations, and intrigue was up and running; their own little shop on the corner was now open, and it would never close.

By the time of Loyola's death in 1556, his priests were working in India, China, Japan, and the New World (America) as well as in France, Germany, Spain, Portugal, Italy, and even subversively in England, with many of the priests arriving on its shores by way of Ireland, in disguise and in many cunning ways and means. "The Holy See emerged strengthened from the crisis where it nearly floundered thanks to the steadfast actions of the Jesuits... politics are their main field of action, as all the efforts of these directors concentrate on one aim: the submission of the world to papacy," wrote Edmond Paris, and nothing much has changed since then.

A well-known quote somehow attributed to Loyola declares that: "I will believe that the white that I see is black if the hierarchical [Catholic] Church so defines." In other words, what the pope commands I will so execute, rather like a faithful cocker spaniel. The veiled depiction of white and black is interesting as well, in that it bears a striking resemblance (does it not?) to the traditional Masonic temple floors of today, and don't forget the distinctive chequered cap bands displayed on most of the world's police today.

So, it's of no surprise that pope Paul III quickly recognised and encouraged this quasi-military order six years after its initial founding. And naturally they would march forward in attacking the Reformation throughout Europe, and of course today the assault against the King James Bible and born-again Bible-believing Christians continues, and not so covertly either.

In his important book *Proofs of a Conspiracy* written by a professor John Robinson and published in 1798, that old professor - possibly a practising but disillusioned mason himself - is so accurate in his statement that the Jesuits were involved in controlling so much of the active masonry in their own lodge uses, then so virulent in Europe.

Here is what he wrote on page 12 of his book: "The Jesuits interfered considerably insinuating themselves into lodges and contributing to increasing that religious mysticism that is to be observed in all the ceremonies of the Order."

Did you get that? It is their own clerical ceremonies and prayers that are being chanted in the lodges. Robinson then goes on to warn that: "This society [Jesuits] is well-known to have put on every shape and to have made use of every means that could promote the power and influence of the order...[they] had hopes of re-establishing the dominion of the church of Rome."

There you are, a future world government in preparation was now on the Jesuits' playing cards, and it was all getting very serious.

He then writes on page 15: "At this time also the Jesuits took a more active hand in Freemasonry than ever. They insinuated themselves into English lodges...at this time changes were made in some of the Masonic symbols particularly in the tracing of the lodge, which bear evident marks of Jesuitical interference...in all this progressive mummery we see much of the hand of the Jesuits, and it would seem that it was encouraged by their church."

So, it seems to me that out of these practising lodges some deep schisms appeared that opened the way for the introduction of the Illuminati in 1776.

Robinson writes on page 59: "Weishaupt [founder of the Order of the Illuminati] had long been scheming the establishment of an association or office, which in time would govern the world to be fashioned in his likeness. In his first fervour and high expectation, he hinted to several ex Jesuits, the probability of their recovering, under a new name."

It seems here there is a rupture somehow in the Jesuit/Masonic connection and Weishaupt would later, it seems, become a marked man, always looking over his shoulder and fearful of the authorities, and of course the ever-watchful Jesuit spies as well. Adam Weishaupt died, we believe, in 1830, and it is claimed he returned/reconciled to the Catholic Church on his deathbed (I certainly hope not!)

Salvation can only ever be found in Christ alone, no church or system!

Robinson rightly called him with almost grudging pride: "The profoundest conspirator that ever existed," and Weishaupt himself would say with bravado to that compliment that: "I am proud to be known to the world as the founder of the Illuminati."

Yet another of his purported sayings sounds more Jesuitical to me in its tone of arrogance: "The human race will become one family, and the world will be the dwelling of rational man." Now, this sounds more like pope Frances and Pierre Teilhard de Chardin. Also making an overture on the world stage of publishing in that momentous year were Common Sense by Thomas Paine and Adam Smith's Wealth of Nations, and all patriotic Americans are aware and some can even recite its passages word for word, this being the Declaration of Independence.

This historical national document was drafted in 1776. Something else momentous was also about to happen that fortuitous year and keep all signed-up conspiracy theorists arguing for years afterwards on the Internet about the Illuminati.

Enquiring Americans should perhaps consider the fact that the Jesuit bishop John Carroll, who presided over the diocese of Baltimore, was the founder of Georgetown University, a building of prestige and power still administered by the Jesuits even today. The Carroll family were also prominent in donating generous tracts of saleable land to construct the growing suburbs of Washington. Its Catholicism was apparently rife, with local residents sarcastically calling it "Rome on the Potomac."

There would later be a dangerous Masonic, maybe Jesuit, influence added to the city's buildings. Early constructions of avenues and boulevards depicting occult magical symbols, and the weird shape of a goat's head situated in the oval office. I wonder what is going on here. Bishop Carroll was involved in building the first cathedral in America, shamefully dedicated to Mary, naturally. Of interest as well is that another Carroll, interestingly a Jesuit-educated scholar, was one of the signers who put his name to the Declaration of Independence, so even there their fingerprints are embossed on this much quoted and loved document. Perhaps the capitol city should have been known as "Carrolltown" and not Washington.

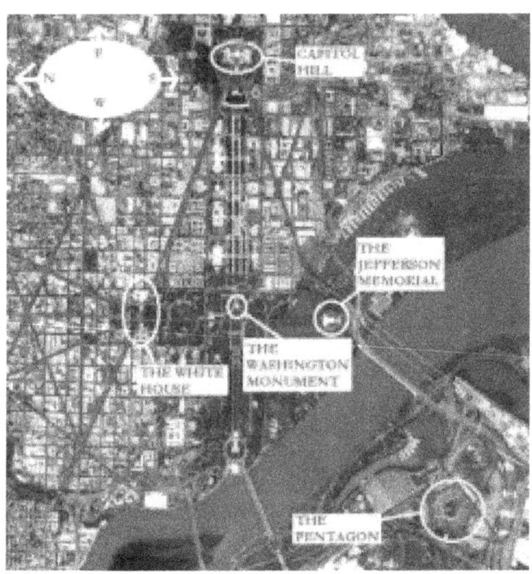

S omeone once remarked and I am not sure who or where: "That I always found it wise to take or steal whatever rights I can get, anywhere, at anytime."

This sounds so much like today's curse of bloated organised religion of which we are all aware and which I try to avoid, with its numerous churches still requesting charitable tax-exempt status; I think it's criminal and should be investigated and eventually abolished.

So, we should perhaps pause and turn to this familiar Bible verse for some much needed spiritual relief and comfort.

Listen to what the Lord says: "Beware of false prophets, which come to you in sheep's clothing, but inwardly they are ravening wolves. Ye shall know them by their fruits. Do men gather grapes of thorns, or figs of thistles?" (Matthew 7:15-16).

Now, to me, that is a severe warning from the Lord Jesus for us to act and pray upon.

Since the conception of the Jesuit order in 1540, there have been thirty superior generals. So if you're sitting comfortably in your recliner, or by the pool, or near the tennis court, then let's begin with discovering more, in my humble opinion, about one of the most interesting of the superiors who occupied that position, namely "general" count Halke Von Ledochowski, a former officer in the old Austrian army and the 26th holder of the Jesuit title of superior general (don't they love their lavish and man-made titles?).

In fact, if you don't mind, I will refer to him from now on as the 30-year-war man or simply the count. It had been his personal ambition, and with the conclusion of two previous popes of course, to construct a new lasting totalitarian "holy Roman empire" in Europe brick-by-brick, then to finally restore, if possible, a new papal Caesar creating a monarch of the world; in other words: "Hail Mighty Caesar!" Naturally, he meant the pope in this Jesuit experiment, and the frightening thing is he nearly succeeded in this experiment. He has previously been described thus: "As a dry dark foxy little man with piercing eyes and a nervous restless manner." And looking at the picture in front of me I can see exactly what the writer was alluding to. He would also boast of a cardinal in his family (an uncle), and a saint of the Catholic Church (his sister), and he would orchestrate a large slice of European history over thirty years in a lively manner, much of it still with us today.

Of course, according to the New Testament, we as born-again Bible-believing Christians are all saints, are we not? And amen to that I say.

The count's tenure of office (and what a page of history it would be) would see him preside over the First World War and part of the Second World War, as well as always being faithful to that most pro-German pope of all times, this being Pius XII, and, "Always suave, emollient, and devious", wrote Edmond Paris.

There must have been jubilation in the Vatican during the first year of the Second World War as Hitler's panzer tanks smashed their way over mostly non-Catholic European borders with little resistance offered or shown to them. By 1940, however, only Protestant England stood alone against the Nazis, yet strangely Hitler hesitated before launching a channel invasion, deciding instead to attack Orthodox Russia; this would be known as "Operation Barbarossa." Of course, he would later regret this military manoeuvre. For England's green and pleasant land, however, it would be a brief respite to rearm, and believe it or not, to hearken to a call by the king for a national day of prayer.

As regards the superior general, Halke Von Ledochowski, hadn't he always cherished the hope that the despised Protestant Britain would quickly capitulate under Catholic Hitler's marching armies in Europe eventually disappearing into the so-called "blitzkrieg" of 1940? The count had already spoken haughtily about the general meeting that the company (of Jesuits) would hold in Rome after England had capitulated.

Well, like so many prelates in the Vatican then and now, hadn't they always referred to Britain patronisingly as "the lost church"?

Now, I seriously want to propose a personal scenario of what might have happened or could have happened if Britain had quickly surrendered and sued for a useless peace, as many in Rome believed and expected to eventually happen. So after a decisive military invasion of Britain to be code-named "Operation Sea Lion," and with the landing by German troops probably on the south coast and perhaps from the east coast as well, the serious business of a brutal occupation would commence for a country not occupied since William the Conqueror in 1066. With newly erected concentration and detention camps and holding barracks very much on the planned agenda, these would have had to be quickly erected with forced slave labour using captured Jews and other known enemies of the Nazi state to begin the task.

Also, it should never be overlooked that a majority of the staff at these hideous death camps in occupied Europe, both militarily and clerical, were predominantly Roman Catholic. We also believe that the bishops of the dioceses where these camps were then situated during the War were aware of this and of what was going on but did nothing. Some British camps were perhaps to be located on the remote Dartmoor Plain and be converted into accommodation for the camp commandant and his family and general staff.

Locations in Cumbria were also suitable spots where internment buildings could be erected very quickly. Perhaps in the hidden glens and crags of Scotland, the same mode of confinement could be erected and some living conditions for the staff could be sited around or near such a barren location.

Also, some holiday chalets prepared for the 'overworked' camp staff could be added with stables and a gymnasium. I also suggest that the count after arrival would have made the triumphant journey himself to a defeated sombre London from Rome via Berlin as a personal guest of Hitler on his private Condor aircraft along with Goering, Himmler, and others of his order along for the ride. But for now, he could savour that precious moment and gloat over the fact that the Jesuits under his watch, who once long ago had been banished from Britain were now back in residence. Oh, and that lost English church was now ensconced into the Roman fold. And I also suggest he would have certainly been chauffeur-driven to the Jesuit Heythrop Hall then situated in rural England, and once there to arrange a champagne gala with a picked nuncio bringing a personal blessing from Pius XII. Also seated at the banquet table would be several pro-Nazi cardinals flown in from the continent to add some colour, displayed in their resplendent robes to this historic occasion of the Reich!

At the Jesuit Farm Street church in London, papal citations would be awarded to devotees of the Holy See no less. Then later that evening a lavish candlelight banquet would be held and hosted by Hitler (but not with Eva by his side), and by invitation only, of course, to be held in one of the magnificent staterooms of Buckingham Palace, with the crown jewels on guarded display. Hitler would insist on that of course. Then the Berlin Philharmonic Orchestra would be specially flown in to play extracts from Wagner's operas with some Viennese waltzes to grace the evening celebrations. Sharing conducting honours would be Maestros Furtwangler or Herbert Von Karajan waving the batons respectively. Later after the "Henkell" champagne toasts had ended and before the dancing commenced. There seated with pride of place would be the Duke and Duchess of Windsor both present as the special guests of the Fuehrer himself.

All of this would be filmed for posterity by Leni Riefenstahl. Some weeks later down at the Mall, Lord Nelson's iconic statue would be replaced on his lofty pigeon-stained column by whom else but Adolph Hitler being illuminated by a dozen Klieg arc lights. Later Trafalgar Square would be appropriately renamed "Barbarossa Square" and just around the corner dear old Leicester Square would be known henceforth as "Horst Wessel Square." There would also be public book burning events (all invited) on Hampstead Heath with all allowed to participate. But bring your own books to kindle the flames. Naturally, all seized copies of the Protestant King James Bible (AV), as well as the books of the Wesley brothers, Charles Spurgeon, and Jewish authors, musicians, and others would be flung on to the flames by cheering crowds of Catholic fascists. All born-again Christians would be arrested and subject to "project fear" with eventual deportations to secret locations, many never to return.

Then daily life (if you could call it that) in Britain would proceed as usual as was witnessed in France, especially in Paris after the shocking defeat of that country in 1940.

Hitler's Mein Kampf and the Jesuit connection!

We now examine the discreet but important contribution in editing the finished version of Hitler's Mien Kampf. This by a sympathetic Jesuit priest named Bernard Stempfle chosen for this task and he, I suspect, would be the count's designated spy as well in Hitler's then frenetic inner Nazi Munich circle. I also suggest that he dispatched by courier some of the rough proofs of Hitler's anti-Semitic ravings in the book to Rome for the count to read, and who knows, make some corrections of his own before giving his final approval.

Maybe Rome arranged a bank transfer for the final printing and later book promotion.

This Jesuit would later be mysteriously murdered in 1934 and maybe this naïve man was aware of too much about the sordid relationship between Hitler and his niece Gelli (who knows?).

So, did pope Pius XI die perhaps by poisoning in 1939? Was the count involved with his slow death? And in 1958 Pius XII had an agonising death too. Was this Jesuit-related as well in his opposition to the agenda of the Jesuit ecumenical council?

I suspect both popes were impervious to what was happening to their church, but it was then under the strict autocratic Jesuit control of the black pope himself.

I don't buy into the suggestion that "mother" Pasqualina was a Jesuit spy in the Vatican, as some suggest. I think she felt too much affection for Pius XII. After all, she had been his housekeeper and confidante since 1917. Now there were other Jesuit spies in the pope's office in 1958, perhaps one of his two Jesuit secretaries might just fit the bill.

The count also collaborated closely, it seems, with Heinrich Himmler's uncle Joseph Gebhard Himmler, himself a Jesuit canon at the court of Bavaria no less. Uncle Joseph would die in mysterious circumstances after the War in Nuremberg prison so it seems he took his Jesuit secrets with him to the grave, very convenient.

It should also be remembered that many Jesuit priests willingly put on the dreaded SS Black Death uniform and wore it with pride, it seems, during the war and obviously with the count's personal approval and encouragement, so writes Edmond Paris. If this is true (and I don't doubt him), then it is truly shocking evidence against a so-called "man of God," which in my opinion he never was. Of course, there were many priests and nuns and other men and women of other religious backgrounds who defied the Nuremberg racial laws of 1935 (Lutheran pastor Paul Schneider for example). They bravely refused to be corrupted by the contagious anti-Semitic Nazi rhetoric of their day, with many being arrested and murdered for a refusal to look the other way. One such man who also said no was Alfred Delp, a 37 year old Jesuit priest who would be hanged in Berlin in 1945. These were truly people of moral steel.

Then Jesuit general, count Halke Von Ledochowski, had conceived a vast plan after the First World War of a federation of Catholic nations in central and eastern Europe forming a unique ongoing espionage spy system. I do wonder if that structure was perhaps never disbanded after the War in 1945 but survived intact and was reactivated by Nazi brigadier general Reinhard Gehlen (himself a Roman Catholic) into post-war CIA-financed-backed spy organisation then operating in West Germany, later to be easily morphed into the BND known as the Federal Intelligence Service.

Then again, as the author Walter Hagen writes: "The Jesuit General count Halke Von Ledochowski was ready to organise some collaboration between the (Nazi) German Secret Service and the Jesuit order." I suspect that the framework of espionage survived the War and still flourishes today. And as the late E. Howard Hunt, former chief of CIA covert operations, correctly commented: "The Jesuits formed the greatest intelligence service in the world, always have." And he should know, I suggest.

Today, powerful unstoppable telecommunications are at an all-time high with surveillance and satellites, and with many companies operating under Catholic CEOs. The Jesuit influence in this growing field cannot be overlooked in their future determination to seize more power for the Jesuit order.

During the count's tenure, now seated at the head table of the Jesuits' high command, he would be involved with the removal of the Romanov family from "Holy Mother Russia," then witness the planned Bolshevik revolution that brought in Lenin to be a newly appointed czar and to preside over Russia with the assistance of the dreaded OGPU, later known as the NKVD.

From Germany (where else?) Lenin, it seems, was secreted into a concealed train courtesy of the German government and bankers with 30 dedicated Bolshevik revolutionaries on board to be met later in Petrograd by Leon Trotsky, another possible Jesuit coadjutant agent. Then there was the attempted early assassination and suspicious death of Lenin in 1924, possibly by poison or syphilis (take your pick), followed by the ascendancy of that previously religious seminarian boy, Joseph Stalin. And was this with the Vatican's approval, I wonder? Was he their future man as well?

Later in Italy the signed treaty with the Vatican with Mussolini's fascists would be completed, and don't forget the invasion of a defenceless Abyssinia with Italian troops being 'blessed' by priests before they marched into battle (rather like that temporal coadjutor cardinal Spellman who blessed B52 bombers in the 1960s before they pounded North Vietnam almost into oblivion).

And were you aware that over half a million people, mainly civilians, were slaughtered in this worthless campaign that mirrored Italy's shame? The count would also witness and encourage, I suggest, the ascendancy of Franco in Spain and

Salazar in Portugal, as well as the rise of his protégé Adolph Hitler. What a ghastly cast of characters, but interestingly we must ask: who was this grand puppet master pulling those purple Nazi Vatican silken strings that allowed so much of this living history to unfold in the 20th century with such terrible consequences resulting in death and destruction?

Well, I can only speculate that the always obliging count aka, "the black pope," fit that religious role. Or maybe he suffered from an impediment of reactive attachment disorder (RAD) that affects so many children well into adulthood? Or in other words, they are completely without a conscience of what they are committing and disregarding the consequences as a result of this affliction!

So, did the count participate so much in the name of his religion and always oblivious to perhaps this psychiatric impediment that he may have suffered from, or was he simply genetically programmed in his deeds, or as they say it's all in the genes? Now, I do not judge the late count (only God will perform that), but I do question his personal religious and political motives, and as well as those men who willingly colluded with him in building and blessing this Catholic new world Hegelian order that left millions dead, homeless, and permanently mentally scared as a result of what he failed to achieve, yet much of what he did achieve remains with us today.

The death of the count in Rome in 1942 by an abdominal abscess is claimed by his church to be the natural cause. But could it perhaps, I suspect, have been by a possible arranged poisoning to permanently silence him to what he had seen or performed at Himmler's Wewelsberg castle, more about this later.

The count was also aware of many Vatican state secrets both of European governments and of his church's wartime financial dealings with each other (always dangerous). We should not overlook the important fact that Himmler's Jesuit uncle was eliminated in a mysterious manner in 1945, and remember he was, after all, just a minor cog in that Jesuit wheel that had run so smoothly until the Wehrmacht were forced to retreat from the doomed Russian campaign in 1942.

Perhaps the count was murdered by a favoured means of poison (perhaps antimony or antipyrine) carefully selected and professionally administered by one of Himmler's S.S. doctors who quickly arranged to visit the ailing count in hospital in the disguise of a visiting priest or friar. And who, I suggest, would ever suspect a cassocked cleric calling on the sick clutching his breviary. Or better still, why not employ the acting talents of an attractive woman passing herself off as a doctor or nurse, or even as a nun secretly arriving in his darkened room to perform the deed with the silent syringe. Maybe she had been loaned out from Mussolini's own secret police (the OVRA) to eliminate the count.

Somebody once remarked rather casually it seems that "the use of poison is a woman's weapon." Well, I don't know about that, but I have to suggest that no one would suspect an angel of death disguised as a nun, or otherwise silently gliding through the hospital wards to administer the ready needle into the count's withered arm, then slowly to usher him from this life unto death.

After 28 years of loyal priestly Jesuit service the count was sadly no longer needed, or as the say "surplus to requirements." But we should not be deceived about what these men have tried (and are still trying) to do to usher into this Luciferian state of sin and shame. Yet God will not be mocked but will summon each of us to give an account of ourselves of all thoughts, words, and deeds we have committed, including the named and shamed so-called men in black as reported in this book.

Chapter 4: "The Count And The Castle"

This logo looks almost identical to Ukraine's Nazi Azov movement

By 1939 the Jesuit influence had now taken a firm foundation in most of occupied Europe, and at the war's end, it had not been breached.

In Spain, the Catholic Church hierarchy had quickly recognised the fascist Franco regime (no surprise there) 20 months before the civil war ended in 1939.

Salazar had Portugal in an iron grip as well as Austria; France was also under a Jesuit church menu.

In Italy, Jesuit superior general Halke Ledochowski had surprisingly appointed a Jesuit priest as Benito Mussolini's private confessor. I suspect that priest heard some interesting things in the wooden box!

Jesuitical influences were also introduced into the lives of people in Belgium and Slovakia. This latter country is of interest to me, as the serving president and briefly prime minister during the war would be a Catholic priest named Joseph Tiso. He would be tried and hanged at the end of the war for war crimes, apparently wearing his clerical clothes.

Croatia is also of interest as well. According to the Bigelow report published in 1946 and later released in 1997, it claimed that the then-fascist regime under Ante Pavelic transported some 295 million dollars (and that's by today's standards) to Switzerland during the dying weeks of the war, with the happy assistance of the Franciscan order, as well as numerous crates of valuable gold coins to the Vatican bank (IWR) in Rome. It seems large sums of currency were despatched to Argentina and Spain, respectively, to aid the so-called "4th Reich," courtesy of the infamous and shameful "Vatican rat run," of course.

You know, I'm reminded of that old gamblers' joke that "Las Vegas was built and prospered on losers." The Vatican bank must have prospered on blood-tainted money stolen from a war-devastated Europe, much of it never to be returned to its rightful owners.

We can only speculate that Heinrich Himmler - the deluded Reich master of the dark arts and the wizard of Wewelsburg sometime before the ill-fated "Operation Barbarossa" was launched against a sleeping Russia - had perhaps decided that a secret religious ceremony should be held and hosted by himself at Wewelsburg Castle. Its purpose, he decided, would be to invite all prominent pro-Nazi priests, bishops and cardinals and quislings of occupied Europe to the castle for a pagan event to call upon their Norse gods to bless this decisive moment of destiny in eliminating the world of godless communism. But it was not to be. Stalin, after some hesitation (perhaps a nervous breakdown, it is claimed), would successfully mobilise the determined Russian people, and the obliging Orthodox Church clergy (what was left of them) to repel the invading Nazi war machine. Later, of course, the tide of war would be turned and much of it would go into Russian future mythology, still spoken about today as the Great Patriotic War.

But what would be more appropriate at the War's cessation than to introduce a new world order out of the smouldering ashes of the old dying world order in 1945. We should also remember that in 1954 the infamous Bilderberg group was introduced to a recovering world by Prince Bernhard of the Netherlands, with other Illuminati suspects.

NATO would later spring into defence mode in 1949 against Stalin. Now they have massively expanded against another Russian, this time Putin.

Interestingly, from another Benelux country and on the 15th September 1946, the 27th superior general of the Jesuits, a certain Jean-Baptiste Janssens, a cold-war warrior priest, some noted, and as the so-called "black pope" certainly ruled over his church during the massive dangerous nuclear arms build-up of the 1950s and 1960s.

He looks like a cold fish from the pictures I have seen and maybe he was involved with the murder of President Kennedy in Dallas with the assistance of the "military vicar" cardinal ('Franny') Spellman, so claims an American author.

(Jean-Baptiste Janssens)

He was also a fanatical devotee, worshipper and promoter of the cause of Mary, so beloved by Rome today. I also suspect that the Jesuits heavily influenced the 1950s Vatican pronouncement from Pope Pius XII that Mary had apparently been "bodily ascended into heaven upon death" (not in the least Biblical of course, the pope also being under heavy medication during this time, which wouldn't have helped him in making "clear infallible" papal edicts). John Paul II, however, seemed to dismiss the Medjugorje melodramas with a Polish sniff; I wonder why!

Interestingly, author and former Catholic priest Peter De Rosa writes in his book Vicars of Christ concerning the bogus "assumption" that could not "his holiness (I detest that made-up title) who declared infallibility in 1950 that a Jewess was taken up body and soul into heaven have said authoritatively in 1942 that her race was not to be annihilated for being Jewish? What prevented him from saying publicly that Catholics cannot participate in mass murder?"

I also noticed the unpleasant Jesuit review on the back of my paperback book that reads that it is: "A binful of garbage."

Perhaps "Hitler's pope" had always had a loathing for the Jews and their race anyway and hindered their survival during the dark days of the War, or was the loathing of the pope and his predecessors before him simply because the Jews had crucified Christ? But in fact, it was the Romans who scourged and crucified Christ, aided and abetted, of course, by Caiaphas and his evil and apostate temple followers, all wicked and unsaved men.

This Vatican belief was taught to my parents at Catholic schools decades ago (before Vatican II), so then perhaps according to the Jesuits' logic, the terrible holocaust initiated by the Nazis (most of whom were Roman Catholics) with the connivance of the German Jesuits as well, would be a simple "payback" time.

Some years ago, I visited Salzburg, Austria, to do some street work and I well remember the old Jewish quarter and the so-called "Jew Street" that operated a curfew for the Jews from dusk 'til dawn. So, it's no surprise that this was initiated and allowed to function with the full knowledge of the Austrian Catholic Church for hundreds of years back then.

When Austria came under the jackboot of the Nazis in 1938, the country then under the Catholic Dr. Seyss Inquart and the support of cardinal Innnitzer of Vienna could well have seen the legal reintroduction of the old "lock-up" curfew being reintroduced in Austria against the Jews, and as such, did nothing about it. Only this time, they didn't just confine the Jews to the degrading "Jew street" by law, but shipped them out via a cold railway cattle truck to Auschwitz for extermination!

However, Himmler's fanatical font of mysticism would not be situated in pagan Rome or the holy city of Jerusalem, or even Mecca, but in the triangular brick-constructed Wewelsburg castle. Now, the Reichfuhrer had previously signed a one-hundred-year lease (can you believe?) in 1934, bringing this historic building into the bulging S.S. portfolio built up on theft and murder.

Previously constructed in the 16th century and in that ancient land of the Saxons near Paderborn, it would be expensively furbished to the requirements of the S.S. and their master Himmler. Much of this would simply comply with his neo-pagan esoteric mythological beliefs as well.

Because external and internal additions were later needed, slave labour from Niederhagen concentration camp would be marched into the site to complete the expensive additions with many camp inmates of course working and suffering in appalling conditions. It is said that when the castle was finally completed, all of the unfortunate workers were quickly taken away and murdered by S.S. thugs. This would be to achieve silence of what they had seen and heard.

Situated in the Paderborn Catholic archdiocese, I do wonder if perhaps the working clergy in chancery knew of what was happening in their diocese or cared about where victims from the above work camp were being supervised and later murdered by Catholic military.

In 1941, archbishop Jaeger (later cardinal) would be appointed by Rome as the new representative of the diocese. He was a frequent guest at the castle sipping Earl Grey tea with Himmler (but not hearing his confession I believe, even though Himmler was a Catholic).

Jaeger had previously served in the army as a military chaplain; then later at the summoned Jesuit Vatican Council (1962-65), he would assist with other liberal socialists in promoting a full seasonal ecumenical program, with the late Jesuit cardinal Bea at the ship's helm. Looking back, it all seemed to have panned out so easily for these communist sleepers, as I well remember.

Those progressive priests/cardinals in Rome demanded friendly socialist agenda to "jazz up their church." The inner rotten core of the Vatican must have been so surprised that so little opposition was seen or heard from parish parishioners or area bishops as the noxious ecumenical papal poison filtered down to the church pews and spread into apostate Christendom.

Wewelsburg Castle would be Himmler's designated pet "Camelot" and there he could entertain his knights of the Reich and guests, perhaps reliving the fables and glory of that celebrated round table and that lost Wagnerian Holy Grail musical world that is so enamoured in German folklore devotees.

An interesting note of interest is that in the dark cellar of the west tower a private bomb-proof safe transported from neutral Switzerland (where I suggest millions of looted dollars and stamped gold bars "requisitioned" by Nazi high command still lies in dormant accounts, perhaps waiting to be activated in that beautiful land of the Alps) had been installed within its foundation. When finally completed, this would then be secured under a handpicked armed guard. Only Himmler and the captain of the castle guard knew of its private combination, or so we are informed.

I do wonder what dark secrets it held in its customised black velvet fire-proof compartments, and what eventually happened to its destination after the War's end when the safe mysteriously disappeared, as did so many other secrets of the Reich.

So, did this elusive secret safe contain perhaps the names and foibles of prominent Jesuit clergy and other government VIPs who had willingly participated in the mock religious ceremonies performed in the so-called "hall of the supreme leaders" of the castle? I do wonder what else it contained.

Of no particular interest, I suppose, is the reported news release that in 1936 an unknown aircraft or UFO as we would call them today crashed into the dense black forest near Freiburg, Germany. It seems the recovered aircraft was then secretly transported by the S.S. officers to the Wewelsburg castle's numerous mechanical workshops and laboratories for an examination. Um, well I wonder what the Nazi German scientists learned of its structure and advanced technology and how it could perhaps come to the aid of the Third Reich in the final dying days of the War. And was this possibly a precursor of the many strange unidentified German aircraft as witnessed in the dying days of the War that seemed to baffle the allies then? Or did that anonymous aircraft perhaps contain interested travellers from the Jesuits mysterious "omega point"? (another clerical belief/myth later to be examined in this book).

Internally, this now-bleak historic former residence of the pampered prince-bishops of old features twelve high-backed thrones set against an inner wall near other medieval artefacts housed there.

Below in the crypt and placed in the centre of the granite floor it is also possible to see a black sun disc. From its fixed centre, twelve runic lightning bolts explode from its centre. Then concealed in the marble setting there was a concealed gas pipe offering an eternal flame (a terrible vision of hell, I suggest) to the "knights" seated around it. Perhaps some form of a drug-induced state brought on by wine or narcotics being offered would then take effect as they revelled in their sins before and after the mock Luciferian Nazi occult practices destined, as always, to transfer those who willingly committed them to the deep crevices of an appointed hell.

Now, I suggest a personal scenario that might sound strange to comprehend today but we must remember that in the 1940s these were strange drug-fuelled times for all in German authority and in England as well. Only today as I write this, the national press reports that most of the Nazi high command during the war were addicted to some cocktail of narcotics. Hence, we note that the Nazi army was able to steamroll their way across most of Europe in 1940, conquering and dividing most of Europe on the way. These mixed potions were called "wakey, wakey drugs" and generous doses of "Pervitin" were brought into the mix, apparently issued to most of the marching troops whether they requested it or not. Absolutely amazing to know about! We have to wonder just what was served up on silver-monogrammed chafing dishes by silent S.S. flunkies at the castle when Himmler's invited guests arrived for a full religious ceremony to an evening reverently prepared with papal pomp and Nazi narcissism.

Never mind "Castles in Spain" or "Castle on the Rhine" or any of those other famous pile of bricks so favoured by horror filmmakers of the past. Wewelsburg was definitely the location to be seen at for the select Nazi elite, I suggest.

But I now suggest seriously that on the anniversary of the death of King Henry the Fowler in 936 AD, Himmler had always had an unhealthy interest for the king and his memory. In fact, he believed he was the supernatural reincarnation of the king. Incidentally, Hitler shared the same delusional view that he had a spiritual supernatural contact with Frederick the Great, and didn't I read that Jesuit-educated Joseph Goebbels rather likened himself to the late tango dancer and silent film star Rudolf Valentine. Ah, the vanity of men!

On the evening of the anniversary or thereabouts of the late king's demise, a religious ceremony of sorts was being performed before the invited guests. It was saturated in the occult tradition of reverence and worship with a black mass being sinfully choreographed in the background of the evening's late night proceedings.

These guests, perhaps inebriated with dangerous concoctions or whatever they had tasted, would invoke the aid of those Norse gods of old, many being derived from Wagnerian Opera and perhaps a small concealed orchestra would be heard, adding to the evening's ambience. However, before the Nazis prepared their attack on a "sleeping" Russia in 1941, many prayers and laments would had been offered up in the void of the castle. Perhaps to Thor, Odin, Magni or Vali. Of course, they all had their favourite gods that evening and all demanding - in their own inimitable manner - an all-out victory over godless Soviet communism.

In the first months of that failed assault, three million German soldiers, all completely ill-prepared for the coming bitter winter, stormed their way across the steppes and villages of a mainly defenceless Russia. This must have felt ecstatic to the pagan Nazi high command back in Berlin and Berchtesgaden in their belief that their false gods had heard and answered their pitiful prayers. Later at the castle, however, on king Henry's anniversary could there have been some notable robed Jesuits and other high echelons of the Illuminati, I suggest, concealed and watching the evening's festivities from amongst the heavy embroidered drapes of the chapel pews that evening? Or maybe Hitler himself and Eva Braun had made a brief unannounced appearance. And perhaps more importantly, Himmler's Jesuit uncle and the Jesuit superior general the count himself, who would have journeyed from Rome for this evening of worship, perhaps to preside and participate in the ceremonies that evening? Who can say whether he was there? I'm sure he was personally invited by Himmler to attend.

Yet during that evening of sin and Satanism, something terrible and abnormal in appearance materialised as the liturgy to the gods was being recited. It arrived out of the shadows of the castle in the so-called castle chapel. It was not a divine apparition but a demonic image from the dark pits of hell.

Within minutes (it must have felt like hours to horrified spectators), the shape of a deformed man - if that's what it was - appeared, then slowly moved forward leaving a disgusting trail of vapour behind itself for all to see and smell, moving erratically towards the frozen terrified guests and with open arms and a deformed face before them.

Instant panic descended on the fleeing revellers. Perhaps some died instantly that night of shock and some were mentally unbalanced for the rest of their lives. Naturally, the count and his entourage quickly slipped out of the castle aided by Himmler's trusted officers, then beat a hasty retreat to Rome, never again to return to that corrupt castle. Five months later the count was dead!

Some claim his mysterious death was by murder. But by whose hand I wonder? So much of the Jesuits' deeds are shrouded in secrecy and scandal, and with the death of the count "this sinister secretive character," as one who remembered, had finally departed to stand before God and give an account of his deeds. But the Jesuitical army would march on to a greater success in the coming cold war years under Jean Batiste Janssen, the 27th superior general. He would castigate the Jesuits in the late 1940s by reminding them that they were: "Not to be allied with the rich and the capitalists." This sounds like pure Marxist/Engels talk to me. Much of this belief would later be grafted into the socialist Catholic "liberation theology" dross so championed and admired in the 1960s by Pedro Arrupe, the 28th superior general of the Jesuit order.

Yet from that bleak Paderborn castle, Heinrich Himmler would initiate his lasting legacy to a dying Europe by bequeathing his selected serving cadres of loyal followers to be known henceforth after the war as "the knights of

Wewelsburg." Their adopted military-religious motto would read in bold gothic-type print: "To be silent but see all." They would successfully stride into post-war Europe and beyond, always an important thread of Himmler's Wewelsburg legacy.

Their presence continues to be known and felt in the secretive world of finance, politics, and the Catholic church of course, and the mighty arm of the military to be later located in Brussels, Moscow, Washington, and London, and maybe reaching into the "tiger" economies of Beijing and Singapore, so important in today's turbulent money markets.

So, who were these so-called "knights"? Perhaps an extension of the long arm of the Jesuits or the SS? It's difficult to say because both were so entwined with each other during the War and afterwards. I suggest these past predators from Paderborn would quickly influence the post-war new world order as well as witnessing the demonic globalisation of the United Nations then waiting in the wings in Manhattan, New York, to preside over the landscape of that city that apparently "never sleeps," in the completed building kindly donated by John D. Rockefeller finally erected over a 17-acre slaughterhouse in 1947. Um, an interesting location I suggest, and all today under the direction of the popular Jesuit Pope Francis, have you noticed?

That castle in Westphalia still stands rather daunting and defiant, weathering time and all of God's elements hurled at its battlements, rather like the Jesuits today, I suppose.

In fact when I first wrote this publication in 2016, the Jesuits in Rome announced their new superior general, the 31st in fact, being the 67 year old Arturo Sosa Abascal from Venezuela, a "political expert," it is claimed, and wearing a sporty moustache (he rather looks to me like the actor Dick Van Dyke of Mary Poppins fame)

The "black pope" meets the "white pope" but who's the real boss?

The political/economic/religious intrigue under this man will continue against those who oppose the Jesuits' blasphemous rule, and we must not forget that the late Hugo Chavez was the Jesuits' puppet until he fell from grace in that country. Now, that poor country is starving and asking for food parcels to be sent to them. So much for Jesuit/socialism, I say. But at the time, Venezuela was a test pilot for world socialism which has failed miserably, as we all know.

Recently the castle experienced a 5-million-pound revamp and I suspect that Himmler would have definitely approved of this spending of the German taxpayers' money, but of course, he would have made some of his own superstitious additions, especially in the "knights" royal throne room, I suggest.

I personally believe the castle should have been demolished at the end of hostilities in 1945.

But all of this is superfluous anyway today without the love and saving grace of Jesus Christ because He is our eternal future, and the Jesuits are just a bloodied page of Catholic church history, and any future without Jesus Christ is indeed bleak indeed.

Always remember: "Whosoever believeth that Jesus is the Christ is born of God" (1 John 5:1).

Are you born again and trusting in Jesus Christ alone to save you? If not, then your future is void and you are eternally lost! You will not hear this soul-saving message from the Jesuits. Only social good works, they proclaim, will offer you a single ticket to heaven. Lies, all lies!

Please read Revelation 20:11-15 for inspiration if in doubt of what is to arrive:

"And I saw a great white throne, and him that sat on it, from whose face the earth and the heaven fled away; and there was found no place for them."

And no mention, did you notice, of that fabled coming Jesuit illusion known as "omega point."

Chapter 5: "Their Hidden Role In Secret Societies"

Reported skull of Ignatius Loyola or Francis Borgia

No study or scrutiny of the Jesuit journal of jostling in the Catholic Church can exclude the introduction of the infamous Illuminati (and yes, we have all heard of them, haven't we? Some claim it derives from a secret Muslim cult known as "Roshaniya"). And of course who is its illustrious founder and more importantly what were their future aspirations and aims for us all through the secret societies of today that still flourish, although mainly covertly?

The Illuminati had been introduced to Europe in the mid-15th century, it is claimed, and always practicing in the sinister use of the occult, witchcraft, perhaps alchemy or hermetic magic, and attempting through meditation and probably drug-induced sessions and maybe orgies to allow these privileged gentlemen to seek the "true light," whatever that is.

As Professor Robison noted in his book on their dubious role in this infamous organisation: "Adam Weishaupt was the founder in 1776 and Weishaupt had long been scheming the establishment or order which in time should govern the world." Now this next extract from his book is interesting to me and it reads: "He hinted to several ex-Jesuits the probability of their recovering under a new name the influence which they formerly possessed and of being again of great service to society."

He had, it seems, originally wished to call this group "the society of perfectibilists." It is a mouthful, I agree, and it seems he was seeking some perfection, but how can you govern and change society through this? I am not sure. The aim of the order, it seems, was to abolish Catholicism and overturn all civil government through one's membership to freemasonry: "Weishaupt had already learnt from his time with the Jesuits the benefit of running a disciplined organisation," so writes Michael Streeter.

It's always easier to infiltrate an existing organisation than to set up a new one, of course. Adam Weishaupt seems to have been deeply influenced by the Cathers and others of that ecclesiastical era who left a long trail of blood through the dubious Roman Catholic history. It is no coincidence to me either that Professor Robison named him, "The profoundest conspirator that ever existed."

I also suggest in all seriousness that Weishaupt did infiltrate those Jesuit walls and that he and his chosen cohorts were eventually able to take full command, at least temporarily of that wicked Jesuit ship which today sails under the newly elected Venezuelan "black pope" captain, Arturo Sosa Abascal. And that is perhaps a skull-and-crossbones I see proudly flying from the ship's mast in Marina di Rimini of the S.S. Loyola as it sails through that ecumenical contaminated sea, always searching for religious and political allies to be enlisted into their clerical clutches.

It seems to me that the professor is implying that the Jesuit influence in the then-unfettered Masonic lodges of Europe had been seriously bridged and damaged. Yet earlier, something seems to have gone wrong in Weishaupt's endeavours because as the professor later writes: "After this disappointment, the 26-year-old Weishaupt became the implacable enemy of the Jesuits."

If true, this would be a very dangerous thing to live with, I suggest, at any time, whether then or now. But his ambition somehow survived with his co-ruler assisting in the orders' success, this being the elusive Baron Von Knigge (codename Philo). He would eventually fall out with Weishaupt, claiming he still retained Jesuit loyalties. Or was the baron possibly a police spy (as some have suggested)?

An interesting character of this period is the shadowy Abbe Augustine de Barruel, a Jesuit, who wrote: "That the Illuminati were involved with the French Revolution," and in its political success as an "inner circle," he also called Weishaupt a "human devil."

The baron had always been one step ahead of the authorities, it seems, and I suspect his organisation was involved in preparations for the French Revolution before his own mysterious death in 1796. Paid Jesuit agents may have murdered the baron after he had outlived his usefulness to the organisation in those uncertain times. But I have never been sure of the baron or his motives. Yet the organisation he co-crafted prospered without Weishaupt at the helm and still exerts a lasting influence in the corridors of power today, and in the shadowy financial-commercial world.

Someone once remarked disparagingly concerning the Jesuits that: "Lethal they always were. Lethargic they never were," and maybe that's the secret of their lasting longevity, being always spies of the shadows and never revealing their true purpose. Perhaps each previously elected Jesuit superior general adding a further slice of secrecy into the order's black books.

Incidentally, there have been thirty-one generals referred to as the infamous "black pope." One unconfirmed news report some time ago claims that Adolfo Nichols, the then 30th superior general, placed a desperate phone call to president Obama requesting that he cancel a crucial Syria air strike about to be launched. Now if true, it does reveal some of the power the Jesuits have acquired for themselves in today's world of espionage and modern warfare, and all of the pain and terror that brings in its terrible wake. But as true born-again Bible-believing Christians, we are commanded to pray for those lost people in authority, and yes I know it's a difficult thing to do, and yes, you would rather be making fudge in the kitchen or practising volleyball or your tennis strokes, but you must learn to do it, and always with grace in your heart as well.

It has also been said that the Jesuits wish to enter and exit without being seen or heard, leaving no trace of themselves to be seen or found, rather like a tarantula spider, I suggest. You rarely see it constructing its amazing web, but it's there for all to see, long after the spider has moved out of its home. Yet their planned agenda and ideology is rich in the ecumenical and interfaith movement so popular today, which they have so carefully controlled and choreographed since the 1960s.

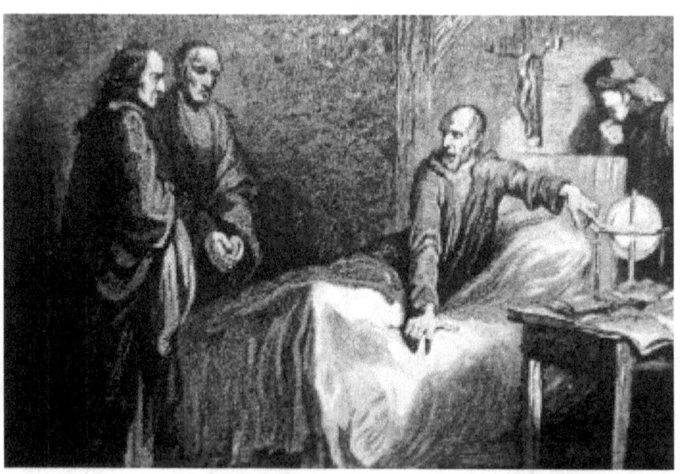

Ignatius Loyola dying

One author, now deceased, makes an interesting observation concerning the French Revolution: "It first began in 1787 or 1789 depending on which book you read. However, it was actually planned by Dr. Adam Weishaupt and the House of Rothschild almost 20 years before the Revolution began. Weishaupt produced the blueprint for it, while the House of Rothschild provided the money." An interesting suggestion that seems to combine Weishaupt and Rothschild working in tandem with each other as co-conspirators and both manoeuvring successfully behind the political/religious shield of secrecy and sin that leads billions to that wide road of despair, death and eternal damnation in Hell.

Yet Weishaupt still remains something of a mystery man today and perhaps that was what he always sought to achieve about himself, he once wrote: "The great strength of our order lies in its concealment. Let it never appear in any place." (The mafia has the same motto).

A fitting epithet for him and his legacy.

Over twenty years ago when I first began researching this shadowy organisation and its then purpose and pedigree in the political arena, very little was known then about its formation or who was pulling its secret strings. It was simply on the periphery of interest to students of the occult or astrology and crime. Today, however, it's gone massively mainstream, hasn't it? And now, it must be the staple diet of all keen YouTubers and podcasters seeking to familiarise themselves and to learn more about the aims and ambitions of this fallen world of Lucifer. But the Illuminati have spewed many fiendish "frogs" out of its own putrid mouth, hasn't it? These were known as the Centre for Foreign Relations (CFR), the Bilderberg Group, the Trilateral Group, the United Nations, Opus Dei which means "work of God," the Knights Templar, the Knights of Malta (with many non-Catholics as members), the Knights of Saint Columba founded in 1919 (my late grandfather was asked if he wished to be associated with them, he declined), and the Catholic Catenian association founded in 1908 in Manchester (they prefer not to be compared to the Protestant Freemasons it seems, well they would wouldn't they!) as well as the well-known Priory of Sion, and the shadowy elusive Eleven, the Brotherhood of the Cross, and the dubious Club of Rome all added to this mix of magic and mysticism as well as the Masons and the Round Table Groups (all wealthy men and women, of course), and most in the pockets of the Jesuits, yet not always aware of it.

Pope Paul VI with Trilateral members

I suppose I should include for inspection the not so well-known B'nai Brith, a Jewish organisation founded in 1843 in New York. However, I ask: are they just a "chummy" convivial meeting group of old boys dedicated to charitable causes for their community? Dr. Freud may have been an occasional guest, it seems, and maybe even Karl Marx. Or is there an elite inner core of power seekers in its midst motivated by power and trying to somehow correct the mistakes of the past?

Of course, I have to naturally spotlight the CIA - appropriately also called the "Catholic Intelligence Agency or the "Catholic Intelligence Actions," as some forgotten comedian once called them in mock horror. I also suggest that so many of the previous serving heads of these powerful intelligence agencies, all long forgotten, have arrived in Washington prepped and prepared from an elitist and privileged Jesuit-educated academic system. One can only speculate that the Jesuits may have invented the popular Facebook for their own intelligence uses, taking in Google and Yahoo along that wide Roman road through the social media outlets including tweets and postings.

It's also worth a mention that before Barrack Obama was elected as a Democratic senator, he had been a paid church employee in Chicago worked closely with a former Jesuit priest, Gregory Galluzzo. It has also been said that the infamous Jesuit institution known as Georgetown University has for some reason become Obama's second home. I wonder why. (Trump would also enjoy a Jesuit connection, studying at Fordham University in the 1960s.) And did not the parliamentarian Edmund Burke remark that, "The Jesuits are an infectious plague." Burke, of course, may be long gone but the "black pope" unfortunately still reigns supreme from Rome in the cloistered shadows of the Vatican.

We are today witnessing the slaughter of thousands of non-Catholics, some born again, some not, who have little to no newspaper or media coverage in the Middle East and elsewhere. To me, this suggests that the late unlamented Spanish Inquisition is being brought out and dusted down all over again with the men in the black masks being the new inquisitors. History always repeats itself, it seems. So it's not so much a war on terror but a war on Bible-believing Christian that seems to continue to this day unabated and wicked, but all of this is part of the end-times scenario, I sadly suggest.

Many other so-called sinister secret societies also exist today, and all usually found lurking in the shadows of suspicion, so mention should be made of a few, such as the Kabbalah. Many early Loyola followers were from Iberia and Jewish in ancestry. Were they perhaps crypto Jews who influenced the Jesuit order's thinking at the time?

The church of Scientology is interesting because the functioning Delphian school today is now situated in Oregon near Sheridan and was a working seminary for Jesuit religious novices until its closure. The scientologists later purchased it in 1976 for their own purposes. Maybe "captain" Ron Hubbard had an admiration for the Jesuits as well, maybe later studying their elusive educational methods to be implemented into the Scientology's timetable of the "study tec."

Do you remember that old worn out Jesuit maxim of "give me a child at seven and I will give you the man"? I think there is something in it, in that we never shake off the old school regime of learning or whoever imparted it upon us, especially from a Catholic background.

The Rosicrucians certainly were Jesuit-influenced and maybe the Ku Klux Klan as well. The name incidentally derives from the Greek word Kyklos, which means circle. They originally were derived from the Knights of the golden Circle" and somewhere in there lurks the dangerous influence of Albert Pike. (The Catholic catenian group also means 'circles.')

The Shriners are also very active in good works, but this will never save the sinner of course, and that can only be gained by faith alone in the precious blood of the Lord Jesus Christ, and any other religious rigmarole is a waste of time.

The Sufis perhaps for consideration, they being cloaked in their worship of mysticism. All of the above groups must be recommended as fertile planting fields for the Jesuits to enter into and inhabit, if they have not done so already, as they have always been active in the Middle East.

The dubious Italian P2 fraternity who may have murdered pope John Paul I, as it has been suggested he had learned of their secret Masonic/occult activities and with some of his own pet cardinals as dutiful members, all enjoying their fringe benefits. The pope had foolishly threatened to expose them, it is claimed. A dangerous thing to attempt. This pope lasted a mere thirty-three days! (33 is very Masonic, for they have 33 levels in their secret religion.)

A later secret society and a "spin-off" from the Illuminati was the strangely named "the League of the Just," or "All men are Brothers." It seems followers of this league attempt to promote and practice what is loosely called "Christian communism." Some notable members who have adopted these utopian tenets of faith would be Leo Tolstoy, Daniel Berrigan S.J. [S.J. meaning "Society of Jesus", the name the Jesuits give themselves], Martin Luther King, Desmond Tutu, and of course the current Jesuit Pope.

Karl Marx, of all people, was approached to update and revise (can you believe?) the earlier writings of Adam Weishaupt by the league. Weishaupt had died in 1830 and was becoming a forgotten man. Karl Marx, with Engels' usual financial support (gained from sweatshops in Manchester), would later graft much of Weishaupt's rules and ravings into his own 1848 Manifesto of the Communist Party. Some doubt Marx's authorship of this political journal, and maybe this document, rather like Hitler's infamous Mein Kampf, was ghostwritten by a Jesuit from Farm Street in London. That's just around the corner from the British Museum that Marx used as a second home, this being suggested by ex-Jesuit priest Alberto Rivera.

Later, it seems, the League of the Just would quietly morph into the communist league, but maybe that was always on the agenda, their political agenda anyway.

The fledgling communists would adopt May 1, which Weishaupt had chosen for the conception of the Illuminati, as their "May Day," and it's still celebrated today. The famous visual insignia would be unveiled as well then, this being the pentagram or five-pointed star. Naturally, it would be coloured red. This, we are informed, "was from the red shield on Meyer Anselm Rothschild's ancestral home."

Now Vladimir Lenin entered onto a nervous world stage already steeped in the mess and mud of the First World War. He had previously immersed himself in the platitudes and dictates of Weishaupt and other revolutionist writers, and of course the socialist propagator Karl Marx. By now, Bolshevism "was on the march and amongst other atrocities, it would terminate a thousand years of the Romanovs' rule resulting in the murder of the Tsar and his defenceless family and cause the Russian Revolution in 1917...they being financed later by both European and American international bankers," writes William Sutton. In fact, American millionaire Jacob Schiff would raise a staggering $20 million using an obliging Leon Trotsky, then domiciled in New York, and himself maybe a Jesuit temporal coadjutor and failed movie actor as a willing go-between of himself and the exiled Lenin.

Incidentally, it seems a prominent Jesuit-educated German minister by the name of Diego Von Bergen was involved in the safe transfer of the Lenin party of communist vipers on that steaming locomotive. He was later politically appointed the German ambassador to the Vatican, of all places, perhaps as a reward for his hard work in this dark deed of the Russian Revolution. The Jesuits had previously perfected their own brand of "communism," it seems, in Paraguay of all places from 1600-1750, being influenced by Plato's *Republic* and Thomas More's *Utopia*. Also of note, More was a bitter enemy of the English Bible translations and was involved in the betrayal and murder of its supporters as well. One can only speculate on the pain and punishment perpetrated on those poor peasants in Paraguay suffering under the religious Jesuit jackboot if they didn't kneel and obey their religious masters.

So why not export it later to Russia in 1917, they must have reasoned in Rome, which they of course did.

There was an unconfirmed rumour that the Vatican had been promised millions of dollars from the Tsar's own private bank, but the Bolsheviks' declined to do this, keeping it for themselves (see the 1917 Tsarist notes with the hidden swastika symbol on display behind the Russian imperial eagle, then of course later Lenin's profile would be displayed on the bank notes).

Rare Russian money, early 20th century

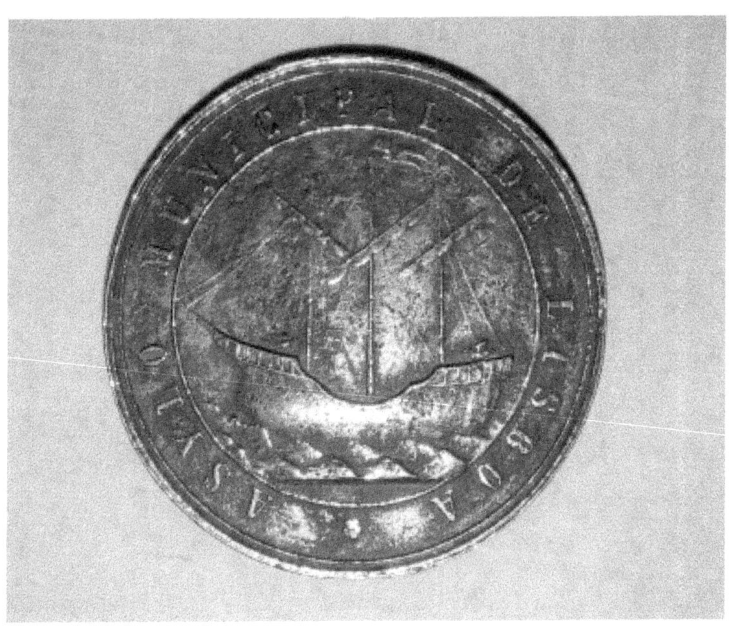

Rare Jesuit Black Ship money, 1802

I don't buy into the mischievous rumour then circulating in Moscow that Rasputin was involved somehow in the removal of the Romanovs. He was always a loyal servant and friend to the Tsar and his family. However, I do point a finger at the sinister hand of Count Ledochowski, the 26th superior general of the Jesuits behind so much of the Russian upheaval of 1917. He certainly knew and directed much of what was going on in those dangerous times in the turmoil of Russia, and what about that well-known Jesuit motto that reads, if you did not know, "Ad maiorem Dei gloriam" (AMOG), or "for the greater glory of God." But one can only speculate which God they owe their loyalty to. I do not believe it is the God of the Holy Bible.

In fact, a Jesuit mass celebrated in Rome recently with the current superior general featured a shaman performing some pagan ritual with fruit and candles, some women shrilling, and a painting depicting (I suppose) the Virgin and Child brought to the altar to be venerated amongst other things and maybe 'blessed.' None of this is Biblical but blasphemous and insulting to the true God of the Holy Bible.

As regards the capitalist financing of the fledgling Bolsheviks as mentioned before: "This has been confirmed by the New York Journal American of February 3rd 1949, that Mr. Jacob Schiff gave 20 million in gold to help push the triumph of Bolshevism in Russia," writes Sutton.

Interestingly, not before being detained in Nova Scotia on 3rdApril 1917, the Trotsky voyage was unexpectedly halted by maritime authorities, but political strings were somehow pulled between Washington and London (perhaps even the Vatican) to eventually allow this revolutionary group of marauders to sail on for Russia. Now listen to this piece of news: "Recent declassified notes by the Canadian government reveal that the authorities knew that the Trotsky party were socialists leaving America for the purpose of starting a revolution against the present Russian government."

This is amazing to read. That the American government were dangerously complicit in removing the Tsar and his government by whatever murderous means, and again I can only speculate where Jesuit general Ledochowski was in all of this world-changing agenda emerging and played out on the European military chessboard and on the high seas.

Was all of this cosy endeavour secretly arranged in a walnut-panelled boardroom somewhere in Wall Street that later allowed Vladimir Lenin himself to be safely ensconced in April 1917 on a sealed steam train leaving from Germany to Russia with his hired henchmen onboard, with all of this covert decision-making being financed, we are told, by Max Warburg, brother of Felix and also Paul of Jekyll Island fame? Interestingly Max Warburg was the manager of the Rothschild/Warburg bank in Frankfurt, Germany.

It's all "very interesting [can anyone now doubt?] that the international bankers were running the whole [rotten] show from behind the scenes", comments author Des Griffin in his interesting 1978 book *Fourth Reich of the Rich*.

To me, the scandal is that these affluent men willingly introduced a godless virus of corrupt communism to later inflict pain and terror and misery on millions of Russians for over 50 years. And of course, the curse of Maoism was to perpetuate even further deep sufferings towards the Chinese people as well as in Castro's Cuba. He seems to have returned to his Jesuit faith in his declining years.

The mutilations and murders of over 100 million people must be placed at the cloistered doors of the Illuminati, courtesy of Weishaupt and his Jesuit co-conspirators leading on to Marx, then Lenin taking in all the other ghoulish communist dictators seen posturing along in the theatrical newsreels of the 20th century along the way.

I just recently came across a disturbing quote from Francesco Borgia, he was the 3rd Jesuit superior general of the order, he boasted that: "We came in like lambs and will rule like wolves, we shall be expelled like dogs and return like eagles."

Some interesting phraseology here, don't you think? Sounds like Niccolò Machiavelli about to instruct the New York Gambino mafia family on how to "corner" the entertainment/ movie industry, if they haven't done so already. All of this covert conspiracy practiced with fine precision by the Jesuit assassins today is descended from that wicked era of Babel steeped in the then-secret societies that practiced sorcery and sin in and around that infamous tower.

Two of the most exclusive secret societies known today are the Jesuits and the college of cardinals, all men of course, and all Catholic. Seems to me these clerics in cassocks will control this fallen world until the Lord returns in triumph with His true saints. But until then, the spiritual survival will be difficult and dangerous. Then the Lord will reign in glory from Jerusalem, the future capital of the world, and guess what: there will not be a pope or cardinal in sight!

Concern should be highlighted education-wise, I suggest, of the assorted past alumni of the Jesuit institutions Fordham University and Georgetown University and also Duquesne University (not Jesuit), and the Jesuit Santa Clara University, and of course the rarely mentioned Jesuit Fairfield University in Connecticut. Many notable alumni would feed into important government positions after graduating from these "temples of learning."

I'm also reminded of Hosea 4:6 that reads: "My people are destroyed for lack of knowledge." And what about those rarely mentioned in the secretive papal bloodlines that have survived and come into the religious equation for almost a thousand years. Many of these "royal" families have served in the Vatican as cardinals, archbishops and popes, all existing and serving in today's papal court.

Ignatius Loyola's ghoulish interest in skulls

An interesting fact concerning the "royal" families of Italy was the previous marriage of David René de Rothschild to Princess Olimpia Anna Aldobrandini, an apparent merger of these two families. A previous Aldobrandini had became pope Clement VIII in 1592. Another prominent Roman family of merit would be the house of Orsini. They would propel three popes of their own into the Vatican papal throne of intrigue and sin.

I have read somewhere how each Jesuit provincial must provide a written daily/maybe weekly report to Rome of what is occurring in his own province. This is also a mandatory feature that the Jehovah's Witness pioneer elder is expected to perform in his daily/weekday report to the Watchtower HQ in Brooklyn, New York although today that organisation is operating out of Wallkill, New York as well as Warwick.

The Jehovah's Witnesses mammoth HQ building has been valued at a staggering $1 billion did you know. Whoever said there was no money in religion? The value of the Jesuit society is unknown, yet the Catholic Church has been valued at billions of dollars, so the Jesuits' own portfolio cannot be dismissed as trivial.

There is an old saying that I heard somewhere that suggests, "The best kept secrets are the ones hidden in plain sight."

After five hundred turbulent years, the Jesuits have infiltrated and reorganised so many of the secret societies that we know about. With present clergy membership of 19,000-21,000, most of the senior principals of the order would have voluntarily recited that hideous 4th vow spoken after the three other vows of poverty, chastity, and obedience to their commander-in-chief, the pope.

The Jesuit brothers are also important in this glue of their order with maybe a select order of Jesuit sisters rumoured to be introduced. Are you aware that the Jesuit brothers today man the powerful telescope in Mount Graham, Arizona, day and night as they roam the galaxies looking for the coming "omega point"? But, sadly they are not looking for the coming of the Messiah, the Lord Jesus Christ, it seems.

For the first time in that church's controversial history, a Jesuit pope and a Jesuit general secretary have arrived from South America and are now ensconced in Rome. And who knows what future plans these two bachelors are preparing behind traditional closed doors. These men are not divine but dangerous to the real born-again Bible-believing Christian. And does not Revelation 18:4 warn about a global disaster, and how all Catholics and other professing believers are to make a quick and permanent exit to the chancellery door. The warning states: "Come out of her my people, that ye be not partakers of her sins, and that ye receive not her plagues."

You have been warned!

My questions to all Catholics who may hopefully be reading this book is quite simply the following: Was it not the terrible Inquisition that slaughtered millions by papal decrees? And what about the almost annihilation of the defenceless Cathers prior to that, in 1229, executed on the pope's so-called "infallible" orders (and with gusto, it seems)? And we should also mention the known historical collusion of Pius XII with Hitler's henchmen that resulted in the planned holocaust of millions, as well as the later devastating AIDS epidemic of the 1980/90s in America when over 400-500 serving priests died from AIDS-related illnesses (one bishop who perished of the virus had his name and occupation changed on his death certificate!!), with many more living with HIV, it has been claimed.

The Catholic church (or as it should be called, the church of Constantine) apparently was in denial about all of this plague, but listen to this: "The church did not want to admit it," this according to Maureen Fiedler, director of "Catholics Speak Out." Now that's a new publication on me.

We would be amiss if we didn't highlight the recent scandals of wicked paedophile sex perpetrated worldwide by Catholic priests, nuns and monks. And all personal incriminating evidence to be concealed in this religious "cover-up" by the Catholic hierarchy often, it's claimed, dispatched in secret diplomatic pouches no less. These sordid shameful scandals will remain a justifiable condemnation of the callous church that represents the court of Constantine.

Even today global earthquakes and tremors and other financial media rumblings as reported are arriving at the walls of Rome. So when will you listen! Isn't this enough for your sceptic minds to heed God's foretold judgment that will descend swiftly on that bloated church that sits astride the infamous seven hills of the so-called eternal city. Do not be deceived, time is short, eternity is forever!!

Chapter 6: "Two Disgraced Jesuits – Pedro Arrupe And Teilhard De Chardin"

Pedro Arrupe on left, Teilhard de Chardin on right

In this final section on the role of the Jesuits in shaping society and covertly influencing the lives of millions of their own Catholics, there are some lingering issues concerning these men in black that needs to be addressed.

Some years ago this message or graffiti was scrawled on a wall in Ulster, Northern Ireland. It read: "Speed limit 30 mph – Jesuits keep out!" No love lost there, it seems! And we all recognise the hideous skull-and-bones image also seen in Jesuit rites, and used of course by the Nazi S.S. officers on their distinctive black uniforms designed by the late Hugo Boss, no less. And yes, that company's merchandise is still being marketed successfully in shopping malls today.

In the educational realm, there is a well-known saying: "Give me a child until he (or she) is seven, and I will give you the man (woman)." This is alleged to have been spoken by Francis Xavier, co-founder of the Jesuits and still heard today. And many alumni from prestigious Jesuit religious universities worldwide have reached into government, industry and banking and have left their mark, of course, and more importantly have become Jesuit temporal coadjutors.

I now want to digress in this Jesuit appraisal to recount that in early 1940 William Donovan, then head of the OSS that would later morph into the CIA, employed the espionage talents of a Belgium Dominican priest, Felix Morlion (never forget that this appalling "religious order" murdered millions during the terrible Inquisition period!). Morlion would act as a bridge between himself and the Vatican intelligence service to strengthen the Vatican espionage division at the time. Later Morlion, with the aid of Donovan, would hastily aid the escape of Nazi agents from occupied Europe by giving safe passage, probably arranged by Donovan himself, to sail to New York, there ensconced under the safe roof of Cardinal "Franny" Spellman, known to his friends as "the Vatican pope".

Yet after the war, ex-CIA director Victor Marchetti remembered: "The CIA very early on made a decision that the Nazis were more valuable as allies and agents than as war criminals." This is a shocking and yet not surprising statement that the CIA would collude and employ former murderers and criminals. After the war, Reinhard Gehlen (one of Hitler's prominent spymasters and a Catholic) was involved with many dubious dangerous activities and murders on that terrible Russian eastern front. He would later be awarded the Sovereign Military Order of Malta by the Vatican. I wonder what his services to the Vatican were in those war years that he should be thought of so highly by the then pope Pius XII! He would later go on to head the post-war German Intelligence machine (BND until 1968). Some claim it was set up with U.S./CIA money.

Here is another interesting quote I found: "The great strength of our order lies in its concealment. Let it never appear in any place in its own name." This apparently is attributed to Adam Weishaupt, the German founder of the infamous Illuminati, but you know it could have been uttered by any of the 30 previous Jesuit superior generals over the last 500 years. In other words, the song is ended but the melody lingers on, does it not?

We need to examine briefly the lives of two men, naturally both of them Jesuit priests. It's interesting, as well, that there have been no English or American Jesuits taking that prominent role in Rome. One exception was a man who looked after the shop during Pedro Arrupes' illness: a liberal American Jesuit by the name of Vincent O'Keefe. But he seemed to fall foul of pope John Paul II's temper for some reason, being quickly disposed of by the pope, who instead installed his own pet

Jesuit to lead the Jesuit order during Pedro Arrupe's ongoing illness.

"Pope John Paul showed how much he mistrusted the society by appointing his own personal delegate," writes William Barrett S.J., and Pedro Arrupe (the serving 29th superior general it is reported "wept [being] overcome with grief when he heard of this extreme intervention" by his boss. Ah, who once remarked that religion is not a cruel master controlled by these duplicitous religious reverends?

If you're trapped in their clerical clutches, get out of it now! Show them the door and become born again and washed in the blood of the Lamb.

It seems there have been some minor "tsunamis" in and out of the Jesuit household kitchens in recent decades. Even the present pope, it seems, as plain "father" (not Mr. Bagglio) appears to have been subjected to the well-known "clergy cold shoulder" (whatever that is) by his own Jesuit superiors.

For him, these were painfully referred to as: "The disgrace years." This all happened long ago in that tumultuous era of the 1970s. It seems that the old boy was no admirer of some of the Marxist brand of liberation theology, the then Jesuit flavour in Argentina and obviously made his views known.

And what did pope Clement XIV remark long ago about the Jesuits in 1773? With total conviction, it seems, he declared from his elevated throne: "We will abolish and suppress the society" (which he did). A brave man indeed, I say! Even the then Catholic encyclopaedia remarked about this dangerous decision of his that, "It was abundantly justified." A year later Clement was dead for whatever reason, maybe by a papal prescription prepared by the court physician, the usual way then, of course, to dispense of nuisance popes (see the death of pope John Paul I). Of interest to me for no special reason is that he had invited Leopold and Wolfgang Mozart (both Freemasons) to the Vatican, where he would listen with amazement as the 14 year old Wolfgang played from memory for him during the family's tour in Italy.

The conniving architect and master builder of the Second Vatican Council of 1962 was the Jesuit/pope's personal confessor, cardinal Augustine Bea. I rather like to compare him with Don Quixote of Man of La Mancha fame and always with the faithful Pedro Arrupe tagging along acting as the Don's faithful Sancho Panza, with Pedro firing spiritual arrows at traditional edicts of his church, sometimes scoring a bull's eye (like the Latin mass), and sometimes not.

So, let's take a look at this Spaniard who wept when his pope overruled him. And who knows? Perhaps this hastened his own death in 1991.

Pedro Arrupe was born on 14th November 1907, in Bilbao, a Basque by birth, as was the Jesuits' founder, Ignatius Loyola.

He once referred to himself as: "That little man [who] parachuted to the head of the society of Jesus in 1965." Or: "Take Christ out of my life and everything would fall apart," or and rather mysteriously he would claim that: "We have access to certain powers that are denied to others." Um, I wonder what these certain mysterious powers are and bestowed upon the Jesuits by whom? Or is this simply Jesuit hype allowing them to bask in some form of self-importance, or maybe satanic?

As I examine the lives of Pedro Arrupe and Teilhard de Chardin (I once saw his name written as Teilhard de Cardigan somewhere), I realise I am journeying into treacherous terrain and maybe possibly dangerous ground on what I write and highlight for myself about both these Jesuit priests and their wicked order! Yet the Jesuit order has to be examined and in some cases exposed for what they proclaim as their corrupted and perverted brand of "Christianity."

Interestingly, the French philosopher Jean-Paul Sartre wrote of them as follows: "Like the freemasons, the Jesuits are one of the great occult forces that govern the world." A powerful statement from the master craftsman of words that should not be ignored or dismissed as irrelevant. So I shall proceed with faith and fortitude in my research of these men and their Jesuit order.

Both of these men today are treated rather as icons by the Jesuit order and this to me borders on personal idolatry. Some years ago whilst my father was in London doing important ministry/tract distribution with dear friends, he had the rare opportunity of engaging an elderly Jesuit in a brief conversation and he wished it had been extended. However, at the mention of Pedro and Teilhard's names, his eyes glazed over with love and admiration when he explained to him that he was researching their lives for an upcoming project. He didn't seem interested in enquiring why he was attempting such a task, yet he was happy to go back and forth with him over theological issues and sadly not the controversial bloodthirsty "fourth vow."

My father on the right speaks to Jesuit on the left

Strangely enough, the young Pedro Arrupe was also seeking his own vocation in life, something that would initially lead him towards the practice of medicine as a young man, a noble profession indeed.

In 1926 he was invited to Lourdes in the foothills and meadows of the Pyrenees to "examine claims of miraculous cures." It would be a life-changing visit for him, it seems. Of course, Jesuit-controlled Hollywood has over the last one hundred years been very taken with both the shrines of Lourdes and Fatima and others where the so-called Marian apparitions had occurred and made popular later through the medium of celluloid.

By the way, look out for a recent Hollywood film offering us Jesuit propaganda about when the order invaded Japan spiritually, some two hundred years ago. A year later, Pedro Arrupe would swap medicine for the mass, chloroform for the confessional, and a white medical coat for the fitted black religious cassock. He was now on his way in reaching the top job of his order.

The whole perception of the so-called queen of heaven as illustrated at Lourdes and the blasphemous daily devotion of Mary needs to be examined. Mary of Nazareth is not "the queen of heaven;" never was and never would be. However, she certainly resides in heaven but is blissfully unaware of how her name is being disgraced and denigrated through the recitation of the rosary and the sickening and sordid statue worship of her! And what about those ambiguous messages from her it is claimed that we hear so much about and always it seems spoken to frightened illiterate children? Why not appear, I ask, direct a mystical message to an important linguist or Harvard or Yale professor dozing on a sunny afternoon on campus with a latte in his hand? Now he would be able to converse with her in a dozen languages, if not more, in whatever one she chose to use. And maybe even some extinct ones at that, or maybe communicate personally with a top-draw Jesuit cardinal at Georgetown, and wouldn't he love to receive a message from her? Now, that would be interesting to hear about on Fox News or a CBS religious special, but of course, it never happens, does it? I do wonder why. And yes, I am of course being somewhat facetious.

This false Mary can never offer perfection, only pain and imperfection to those who venerate her image. Such a practice has indeed risen from the occult depths, and is both dangerous and misleading as it robs the glory from the Lord Jesus Christ, which of course has always been Satan's purpose. Today over a thousand shrines and grottos are dedicated to "Mary" and all flourishing financially, it seems, showing that he is succeeding. Of course, all will be destroyed when the Lord returns in triumph to detach the apostate church from this fallen world at the Second Coming. Ah, a happy day yet to arrive and yearned for by so many.

The whole controversial cult worship of Mary stretches right back to Babylon and Egypt. In Babylon, the wife of Nimrod was Semiramis, a practicing witch (and there's plenty of them today), and it seems both she and her husband "came up with the idea of confessional and celibacy for their priests."

Eventually, she would be replaced by many other cheap imitations that spread like an epidemic in the Roman world and beyond, such as Indrani and child, Devayani and Krishna, and the cult of worship of these women would eventually arrive to Rome where the unhealthy worship of Venus and others were being fostered. This would later be adopted by Constantine and his mother Helen being promoted through the depiction of Mary, "the queen of heaven." Of course, she was seen many times in art and elsewhere, always clutching the child Jesus in her arms. This would reach deep into post-Constantine Europe and into the Far East.

It seems when the Jesuit missionaries (or as they should be called, agent provocateurs) arrived in their journeys for conversions, many forced, they would be subjected to what they themselves witnessed, later quickly promoting the cult of the Virgin Mary and child. This would later become a lucrative financial purse for the order and church.

Today the Marian shrines of Lourdes, for example, boast nearly as many hostels and accommodation as Paris. Whoever said, "religion doesn't pay"?

Remember: only the Lord Jesus Christ is the saving door to Heaven. But follow the impostor/demon goddess known as "Mary" and that spirit will take you straight to Hell. Hell is never full, always room for one more, so make sure you don't end up there!!!

Through the depraved ecumenical and interfaith movements, many precious souls sadly will perish and be lost forever from the glory of witnessing heaven and all its splendour. There will be no second chance to repent. Tragically for many, it will be too late. But always remember, Jesus said: "I am the way, the truth, and the life: no man cometh unto the Father, but by me" (John 14:6).

So, if you're "cruising" along and trusting in a false church system, you've been warned!!! According to the late Alberto

Rivera, a former Jesuit priest himself, Pedro Arrupe had been a leading "comrade" of the Spanish communist party no less. Arrupe would later remove himself from the Franco regime's clutches, perhaps for political reasons I suggest, departing for Northern Europe, later being ordained in America in 1936. Arrupe had no less than six bridges named after him.

The Jesuit order would later "exile" him to Japan, possibly because of his left political leanings, but it's not clear. He would then spend 27 years in Japan, returning only to Europe infrequently for clerical or family reasons, "and not a soul was saved," remarked the late Peter S. Ruckman concerning Arrupe's long Japanese sojourn. "How true!" we say to that statement.

These Japanese years of Pedro Arrupe are cloaked in confusion and conspiracy, so let's look at some of them, such as: Why were protestant ministers imprisoned in Japan pre the War, yet the Jesuits were allowed, it seems, to go about their business unhindered? Was the atomic bomb detonated in 1945 simply a militarily trial run to be later used against Stalin's armies and a possible planned Pentagon attack on Soviet Russia by America?

Was that coyly named "fat boy" bomb just simply a modified "flash bomb" guided and detonated by Jesuit scientists from their house in Nagasaki? And why was there no deep crater after its apparent explosion, which would normally leave lakes of rubble and debris such as seen in the pre-trial tests filmed in Nevada? These scientific theories have led to the suggestion today that the Jesuits are behind Area 51, the secret base in the Nevada desert. Are the so-called "grey aliens" suspiciously coming and going from that guarded site since 1947, and it is claimed happily living and cohabitating amongst us all without fear of reprisals against them and under presidential protection, perhaps by executive order? They are also known to some researchers as extra-dimensional. I prefer to call them fallen angels. Devils. Demons!

Perhaps this would explain why the Jesuit pope Francis was reported as saying he would "baptize aliens."

So, it looks as if some near future "alien mother-ship arrival " is being sought by the Jesuits, as their many manned observatories (perhaps over 30) continually sweep the heavens with all communication naturally going through this pope and his advisors from his Jesuit order when they effortlessly land – maybe in Arizona or the Nevada desert (yes, Nevada again). If indeed these cold-blooded creatures have been safely domiciled here since the Second World War as suggested by others, then perhaps they are residing in other vast desert wastelands, such as the Sahara (where incidentally snow fell in 2016 for the first time in nearly 40 years). And they won't like that, will they? Or maybe the Arabian or Syrian desert where perhaps those elusive "weapons of mass destruction" are waiting to be discovered one day?

How about Antarctica as an alien base or would that be too cold for them (unless they are residing in pre-heated deep caverns perhaps constructed many years ago by slave labour)? There was a strange religious ceremony, did you know, carried out there in 2016 by the Russian patriarch Kirill and it seems a papal blessing was sought from the pope in Cuba of all places, both unsaved men of course, and maybe Obama made a secret trip at the same time to that unknown region recently. Are they here to aid or annihilate us? That is the unanswered question.

The mysterious Gobi desert should also be examined. This, after all, was Teilhard de Chardin's old stomping ground, of course, and in fact the climate and terrain there would rather agree with these cold-blooded aliens and allow them to construct their own secret military bases in these "hot-spots" of the globe. Who knows? Maybe Teilhard made contact himself with a colony of aliens after so many years roaming that Chinese desert wearing the obligatory pith helmet, in the 1930s searching for *homo erectus* and instead stumbled over some other alien civilisation and certainly more dangerous than what he was searching for?

I have several questions for the reader to consider, which to date, have not satisfactorily been answered by Rome or others:

1) What was the true terrifying story of the naval ship the U.S.S. Indianapolis that was mysteriously torpedoed in the dying days of the Second World War, resulting in the terrible deaths of over 1,000 serving sailors who desperately tried to swim ashore from the sinking ship only to be devoured by sharks?

2) What of Pedro Arrupe's own arrest being charged as a spy by the Japanese secret police where he would later be incarcerated for 33 days (a symbolic number), this being after the surprise attack on Pearl Harbor on 7th December 1941? (It has long

bccn claimed the U.S. government knew of the planned Japanese attack days before it happened. Some of the family of the American high command are still trying to clear their late relatives' names). And why in a short black-and-white news film is Arrupe sitting in an open court with his printed name hanging around his neck? And is that American newspaper men standing in and around him talking? This being when America was at war with Japan, or was this filmed after the War?

Very strange incident indeed.

Arrupe in the dock

3) So much of this period from 1945 in Japan is still "classified." Why?

4) Why was Arrupe exiled so long in Japan and was there an international arrest warrant for him?

5) What does it mean concerning the Jesuits and their loyalty oath spoken to the pope and why did pope Paul VI remark rather ambiguously that the Jesuits "had wounded him." Pope John Paul II went even further when he said: "The Jesuits are causing confusion..."

"The black pope," left, with the *imposter* pope Paul VI, centre

Many of the eastern religious practices, such as the bowing and greeting to strangers with hands joined together, have quietly replaced the old traditional genuflecting, this being known as "inculturation" as witnessed by Hindu holy men or bowing reverently to heathen gods, i.e. as seen in yoga and Tai Chi-Chi Kung.

On the topic of eastern religions, as I finish writing this book, the Dalai Lama is in trouble for asking a young boy to "such his tongue" during a recent public event. The majority of the western media have deliberately looked the other way when deciding not to report this, with others deciding to defend such as a "culture thing." For the record, the Dalai Lama believes he is a reincarnation of a previous leader from almost a hundred years ago! No Jesuit would ever dare question or critique this. (See Hebrews 9:27).

The late ex-Jesuit priest Malachi Martin claimed that the Jesuits had gone "rogue" and no longer, it seems, supported papal progress. He further stated on a radio interview some years ago (1990) that: "The Jesuits have declared a silent war on the papacy" and remember: this man had been a practicing Jesuit for most of his life! Unfortunately, he seems to have died being a dedicated worshipper of Mary, as well as believing and promoting that false region of purgatory of all things. He did also claim: "That Satan is alive and active and should not be ignored." Well, on this point, I fully concur with this alarming fact.

This may be why John Paul II overruled an ailing Pedro Arrupe's wish and suggestion that a fellow Jesuit, the American Vincent O'Keefe, could be proposed to become the next superior general of the order. Well, that's what he wanted but didn't get. Instead, the pope appointed his own pick (an inside man), much to the anguish of Arrupe, of course. Pedro Arrupe expired in 1991, but he had actually resigned in 1983 due to declining health.

His lasting legacy is the "curse" of full-blown murderous liberation theology that assaulted almost all of South America back then, and perhaps from the 1970s onwards. The clerical crime of his Jesuit priests was persuading peasants in deprived countries of the false Catholic belief that religious justice and peace edicts from the Vatican can and could offer a better world to the lost and the damned. Yet Jesus said: "I am the light of the world, he that followeth me shall not walk in darkness but shall have the light of life" (John 8:12).

As a matter of fact, a priest named Gustavo Gutierrez coined those revolutionary words of attack: "liberation theology." But there is no liberation, of course, from the social sin in any theological treatise. Only the precious blood of Jesus Christ will liberate all repenting sinners from sin and more importantly, he/she must become born again. Good works in aiding the poor or deprived through pious works will always fail miserably, and liberation theology with its communist chant to reform or abolish capitalism will always fail. Wealth (like the poor) will always be with us. You will never completely eradicate all the pain and poverty in this fallen world. Of course, all of this nonsense will be eclipsed when the Saviour returns with a fiery sword.

Pedro Arrupe's Jesuit priests and soldiers then toiling in South American jungles and shanty towns had well-worn, well-thumbed copies of Marx's Das Capital and Lenin's One Step Forward, Two Steps Back tucked into their camouflage rucksacks. Teilhard de Chardin, perhaps the father of the new age movement as he has been called, would have memorised Charles Darwin's ridiculous and racist book On the Origin of Species, and I also suggest Huxley's book Man's Place in Nature, or the works of the spiritualist Alfred Russel Wallace.

It's interesting to note the stupid title of the "big bang theory" so widely and proudly promoted today by the left-wing Marxist media was ironically coined by a Belgium Jesuit priest named George Lemaitre.

Well, why am I not surprised that such Satanic mischief-making can be traced right back to this pseudo "Christian church"/order of the Jesuits! But indeed, the Holy Bible states: "In the beginning God created the heaven and the earth" (Genesis 1:1). The hoax of "the big-bang theory" is a Jesuit LIE, whatever this pope proclaims privately or otherwise. God will not be mocked, not even by a serving pope!

Interestingly, Teilhard had been involved with the successful Piltdown Man hoax in 1912 then in England, as well as, I suggest, perhaps colluding with others in the scheme to promote the so-called wonder "Peking man" in China in the late 1920s.

Pedro Arrupe's ambition was to liberate the so-called downtrodden "masses" from the curse of cruel capitalism by force-feeding heavy doses of religious liberation theology of clerical castor oil, always administered from a wooden spoon. And would Teilhard know what "liberation theology" was if he tripped over it on his numerous archaeological digs in Africa and China? Hadn't he always, it seems, had adolescent archaeological ambitions of being the palaeontologist who would find the so-called "missing link" or *homo erectus*? This, of course, was intended to be his silver bullet in later dismembering the Biblical account of Genesis on the creation of man!

Today, the works of the Jesuit Teilhard de Chardin are on open display in Moscow's "hall of atheism" (can you believe?) alongside the mouldering works of Marx and Lenin. Of interest, is that the so-called "Piltdown man" was discovered before WWI, and "Peking man" would disappear shortly before WW2.

According to now declassified CIA documents, in 1935 Teilhard de Chardin was involved somehow with the U.S. Office of Naval Intelligence no less, apparently running covert spies from Shanghai into Japan. According to an anonymous general who had apparently recruited over 30 trained agents besides Teilhard de Chardin, he later claimed that money motivated most of the paid agents (isn't it usually that way?). So here we discover that this Jesuit priest was somehow acting as an unpaid spy or recruiting officer (as far as we know) for American intelligence. What's going on here? What was his motive? Was it possibly, I suggest, because of the generous financial support he and his team had been granted from the Rockefeller organisation? If so, was he then acting under sealed strict orders from his Jesuit superior general Halke von Ledochowski in perhaps assisting the Vatican's own secret service, the Sodalitium Pranum along with other European intelligence services in this spy mix as well?

Today it's difficult to claim or deny, but murky waters are indeed found in this sewer of spies, with somehow a dash of clerical cocktail to sweeten this sour drink. And doesn't it seem to dovetail nicely into the world of organised religion combined with espionage practices into this lair of lies?

It also worth noting that both Arrupe and Teilhard de Chardin seem to have both been banished for whatever reason from Europe by their Jesuit order, and for long periods as well. Again, one can only speculate what the real reason was.

It seems that the familiar finger of suspicion has to be pointed at this palaeontologist priest, amongst other favoured suspects in the Piltdown Man (1912) and Peking Man conspiracy skulduggery theories because: "Teilhard de Chardin had an international reputation as a discoverer of Peking man and Piltdown," so writes Ronald Millar.

So, let's look at some of the popular Piltdown suspects in particular order:

1) Charles "digger" Dawson. This man was an amateur palaeontologist (there were many of them at the time, it seems) and has been credited with perhaps discovering the Piltdown skulls. By profession, he was a dubious solicitor, it seems, and Freemason from Uckfield in Sussex. He also went under the unusual sobriquet of "the wizard of Sussex," not sure why. Well, maybe because of some Wicca activities in that region of Sussex. Teilhard first met him in 1908; however, 40 years later the famed skull was found to be a hoax. Was Dawson the sole hoaxer or did he have an accomplice? A rumour surfaced some years ago that Dawson was being blackmailed, but by whom and for what purpose is not known. Did he perhaps reconstruct a discarded human skull to an ape's jawbone with

filed-down teeth under his own steam then heavily stain the skull? Well, one witness would later claim to recall seeing him engaged in such an act.

2) Sir. Arthur Conan Doyle of "Sherlock Holmes" fame conveniently resided near by the site and was aware of the team of diggers, often pausing to converse with them as he passed by on his way to play a round of golf. He may even have met and talked with Teilhard as well. And I don't see why not. Doyle might have mischievously planted some personal fossils at the deserted dig. He was a collector, after all, and he would later have one of the characters in his book The Lost World (1912) remark rather mysteriously that: "If you are clever and know your business you can fake a bone as easily as you can take a photograph," an interesting coded statement, I suggest, for the reader to work out for himself. He also had a loathing for the Jesuit order of priests, having been brutalised by that order at the Stonyhurst College where he attended for many years as a boy. He would later be taught in Austria under the Jesuits as well and would also become deeply involved with spiritualism. He may have been just administering some personal revenge on that despised Roman religious order of the Jesuits, naturally using a young Teilhard as the bait for his vengeful motives. What a shame about Doyle's faith in spiritualism.

3) Teilhard de Chardin. One man aware of that controversial Piltdown period pre the First World War was a Mr David Essex, a man who himself was living and teaching near the site. He informed an interviewer years later that: "Briefly he is convinced that Teilhard de Chardin was the hoaxer and he did not think anyone else was involved. He believed that Charles

Dawson had been an innocent victim, duped by a conniving French priest."

The author Ronald Millar in his 1972 book The Piltdown Men writes that: "Charles Dawson befriended Teilhard de Chardin, introduced him to the Geological Society and assisted him in making his first big discovery... and that he had been favoured with the skill and assistance of Teilhard de Chardin."

When the skull was finally found to be a forgery in 1950 after extensive fluorine-based laboratory tests, Teilhard de Chardin "preferred not to make a public statement, he then was of course the only person alive who had worked on the Dawson dig long ago."

The late Harvard palaeontologist Stephen J. Gould who "had read all the official documents of the case" was convinced of Teilhard's culpability in the episode and as he saw it and suggested, another view was that "Teilhard's probable motive for assisting Dawson was a curious mixture of nationalistic spite and the irresistible desire to test the gullibility of the scientific establishment," writes Frank Spencer commenting on Gould's findings.

Well, I'm not so sure, so I suggest perhaps Teilhard decided for whatever reason to discover the so-called "missing link" thereby confirming his own religious doubts and bring his ideas to the world, or so he hoped: "Ah, what fools these mortals be," wrote Shakespeare!

It is also of interest to some that the jaw bone fixed to the skull had maybe arrived from a working archaeological site in

Montpellier, France, and of course, Teilhard may have visited that location himself out of curiosity, later secreting the bones to England. The famous tooth that he also discovered "by chance" at the dig in Sussex amongst the rubble and dust and dirt was later said to have come from North Africa, maybe Egypt or Tunisia. Teilhard had, of course, visited both countries previously and resided in Egypt as well. So could he not have swiftly pocketed the tooth as well under the scorching sun, then taking it with him to England, and later suspiciously scattering it at the Dawson dig to be conveniently spotted later (which of course it was)? Amazingly, this simple hoax would survive for forty years until it was revealed years later to a shocked world.

Was this hoax engineered later in China, where bones claiming to be the Peking man were located by Teilhard and his team? That suspicious skull has not survived, having been mysteriously "mislaid" in 1941. Teilhard was himself interrogated in 1941 concerning this skull and its whereabouts by the Chinese police, in fact in the same year that Pedro Arrupe was detained by Japanese authorities on charges of spying or aiding the enemy. Interesting the Jesuit connection again, isn't it?

"Pride *goeth* before destruction, and an haughty spirit before a fall" (Proverbs 16:18). How true! And with the scientific discovery in 1953 proving that Piltdown man was just a clever phoney and with a serious possibility that "Peking man" would go the same way after serious examination, the French Jesuit may have lived in deep fear that he could be professionally named as behind both of these serious shameful hoaxes.

However, "Now old and weak…Teilhard returned to New York. He was sentenced to living out his days in a foreign land," writes Amir D. Acczel.

In a final letter to a friend Teilhard confesses that: "I am still nervous, more nervous than I would, than should be." How sad and I do perhaps wonder what he was nervous or alarmed about. And did all this suppressed fear date back to the dark Piltdown and Peking men periods of this Jesuit's tumultuous life? Who knows!

Teilhard de Chardin died in New York on 10th April 1955 of a massive cerebral haemorrhage, it was reported. Interestingly, after the church (Jesuit) service: "The coffin was taken for burial but the ground was still partially frozen so the coffin was kept in a vault for several days, until a grave could be dug," writes Amir D. Aczel. But of course there will be no frozen ground or lakes in hell, instead, the blistering heat will be far more severe than the Gobi desert, and only in the lake of fire will we see and hear the weeping and wailing of those cast into its fiery furnace one day soon.

Sad old man still searching for "the missing link" and not believing the Bible

The Holy Bible warns us: "Enter ye in at the strait gate: for wide *is* the gate, and broad *is* the way, that leadeth to destruction... Because strait is the gate, and narrow *is* the way, which leadeth unto life, and few there be that find it" (Matthew 7:13-14).

As a committed Christian and Bible believer, I sincerely and humbly urge you today to examine your conscience and repent and become saved. Time is short. Eternity is forever.

Much of Pedro Arrupe's dangerous liberation theology is accepted, perhaps grudgingly, by some clerics in the Vatican and even this pope seems too critical of some of its liberal tenets, and I'm not sure why. Yet theologian Jung Mo Sung suggests that: "Part of liberation theology has been elevated to the doctrine of the church." Um, I wonder what part he is referring to, but it must be always remembered that this conspiratorial church of Constantine is an apostate church, never Biblical, and that their creed is leading millions even now to the gates of Hell.

The apostle Peter would proclaim: "Neither is there salvation in any other: for there is none other name under heaven given among men, whereby we must be saved" (Acts 4:12).

These so-called educated men refused to accept or allow His deity and exclusivity to Heaven to be exposed for glory, rather they enhanced themselves with their own agenda of self-promotion. One Jesuit (Teilhard de Chardin) would happily abandon his life in seeking answers to the world's conception and deny the hand of God in this creation, instead always searching for a trench of bones left long ago baking in the deserts of the world. The other (Arrupe) always seeking an answer to life's problems and mistakenly delving into the fruitless political tomes of Marx and Lenin and others, but never the Holy Bible, it seems.

As John the Baptist remarked so truthfully: "He must increase, but I *must* decrease" (John 3:30).

But these Jesuit men were always false teachers, their religious heresies always infecting so many. Sadly, it is still occurring today all around us. Also, through their wicked ways, these

Vatican assassins have relied on Machiavelli's words that "the end justifies the means" to perform many murders and cause mayhem, inflicting misery on many innocent people. The Jesuits supported a united Catholic Ireland, using the IRA for their religious purpose in that land of my grandfather.

Incidentally, this week is the 25th anniversary of the Good Friday peace agreement that officially ended the long and bloody war in Northern Ireland. Peace at any price is a hard sell to any group of people, especially the vast majority of victims of the almost 3,000 who have yet to receive any justice. Thankfully God sees and hears everything, and one day justice and righteousness will be evident for those righteous souls to inherit upon death.

It's also interesting to me that the Guido Fawke's facemask worn so brazenly today by those who oppose the NWO and globalisation always seem to be sported at any demonstration, have you noticed? Guido Fawkes was perhaps a recruited Jesuit coadjutor involved with the attempted destruction with others of Jesuit inclination and intolerance in the deliberate act of destroying the British Parliament in 1605, but God prevented their destructive devices from succeeding, as He had in thwarting the Catholic-conceived Spanish armada's attack against Elizabeth's England. Six years later, the wonderful and irreplaceable King James Bible (AV) was finally published. Praise the Lord! For more information on this era, please see my two books: Oliver Cromwell | The Last King of England, and King James I of England: The King The Vatican Could Not Kill.

Today the King James Bible is still gaining strength and being sustained through its timeless spiritual message and always offering saving sustenance to those who genuinely seek redemption in its pages. The Jesuits will never hinder or destroy its eternal message from reaching a fallen world. In fact, 100+ million King James Bibles are sold or given away each year, did you know? Praise the Lord indeed for this ongoing blessing.

The archaeological artwork of Teilhard de Chardin never could or would rescue one lost unrepentant sinner in his fruitless wanderings so long ago, be it in the jungle, tundra, or desert. The Jesuits in this book will be judged one day for their past deeds, as will the many other heretics who have aided and abetted with these so-called "priests" of Rome.

Today the ecumenical enigma is being played out in tents of worship. For example, I suggest the so-called "Alpha Course" (curse) is just one. And does not interfaith worship flourish in the quagmire of pagan worship as well? Many churches or temples and even mosques are willingly colluding, adroitly drawing many into their web of false faiths, all of course controlled and expertly managed and mortgaged at the top by the Jesuits.

One day that religious swamp will be drained when the Lord triumphantly descends to this fallen wicked world, bringing the New Jerusalem with Him. God will never be mocked or derided by the Jesuits or any other religious order of men who try to place themselves above Him or His Glory. They do so at their own peril.

It is too soon to speculate where the current black pope Arturo Sosa will direct his future Jesuit attention. I suggest it will not be moral issues, but rather social grievances such as fracking, climate control, wealth distribution, and the eradication of capitalism. But did not Jesus say: "For ye have the poor always with you" (Matthew 26:11)? This is a contradiction on their part.

Apparently, we are told that strange unknown signals are emanating from deep space, and for the Jesuits, this could be a future imminent prelude to an alien invasion or visit depending on your viewpoint.

The Jesuits have longed to see the fulfilment of their pet "omega point" as a cornerstone of their order's beliefs, and a future covenant with these "visitors" (be they friend or foe) would be welcomed by the black and white pope together.

There is however no grey area as regards sin. Even today the pope is hypocritically warning about materialism instead of repentance, and publicly kissing a doll replica of the infant Jesus on Christmas Eve in the basilica in Rome; this looks cheap and obscene!

All must be liberated from sin not financial wealth. Remember: the Lord Jesus came to save those lost to sin who, without His personal sacrifice, would be on that wide road to everlasting hell. Only faith alone in the precious blood of Jesus Christ can save repenting sinners. The Jesuits and their church can offer nothing.

Born again Bible-believing Christians should be more concerned about domestic and foreign terrorists than aliens. And let's not forget the Jesuits' own IHS symbol that proudly adorns their own churches. They are the real spiritual enemy to Bible-believing Christians, never alien beings.

"And have no fellowship with the unfruitful works of darkness, but rather reprove them.For it is a shame even to speak of those things which are done of them in secret.But all things that are reproved are made manifest by the light: for whatsoever doth make manifest is light" (Ephesians 5:11-13).

AFTERWORD

In the spring of 2023, Ukraine's president, Volodymyr Zelenskyy, held high-level talks at the Vatican with the pope and his most senior political priest, Paul Gallagher. During this secret meeting which lasted some 90 minutes, the head of MI6, Richard Moore, was also present. The archbishop in question, Paul Gallagher, is not a Jesuit priest but a member of the Order of Prince Henry, a secret European Catholic Masonic order.

Zelenskyy also broke with official Catholic protocol when he presented the pope with a black silhouette instead of the baby Jesus held by the Madonna.

The president and pope initially posed for the usual publicity shots before the actual meeting commenced behind closed doors with Gallagher chairing it.

The reason for adding this as a late postscript is to once again highlight and emphasise how real-world power has always been in Rome. Politicians come and go, but the papacy does not.

Zelenskyy's Satanic statue is symbolic of how the elite truly feels about the blessed Lord Jesus Christ. But what is more sinful and shameful is how the Vatican, as always, fails to stand against such sinister behaviour and fails to defend the Son of God, whom they claim to love and represent.

Rome was also quick not to remain neutral when the Russia-Ukraine war broke out but sided firmly with Kyiv and not Moscow. The true Church of the Lord Jesus Christ does not take sides but stands for the truth of the Gospel by calling on all sinners everywhere to repent and receive Christ as their own personal Saviour. This is something the Vatican has not and nor will ever do.

Reference books

The Jesuit and the Skull, Amir D. Aczel

Teilhard, Mary and Ellen Lukas

The Piltdown Men, Ronald Millar

Piltdown, Frank Spencer

Teilhard de Chardin, Paul Grenet

The Jesuits, Alain Woodrow

The English Jesuits from Campion to Martindale, Bernard Bassett S.J. and Rodger Charles S.J.

The Secret History of the Jesuits, Edmund Paris

Catholicism Against Itself, O.C Lambert

Europe in the Sixteenth Century, H.G. Koenigsberger and George L. Mosse

Pope Francis: The Last Pope, Leo Lyon Zagami

Exo Vaticana: Petrus Romanus, Project L.U.C.I.F.E.R, Thomas Horn and Cris Putnam

Proofs of a Conspiracy, John Robison

The Meaning of Masonry, W.L. Wilmshurst

The Temple and the Lodge, Michael Baigent and Richard Leigh

The Jesuits, A History, David J. Mitchell

The Search for Earth's Twin, Stuart Clark

Secrets of the Vatican, Cyrus Shahrad

The Uninvited, Nick Pope

The New Age Movement: The Illuminati 666, Roy Anderson

Murder by Poison, Nicola Sly

Hitler's Pope, John Cornwell

Also by James Battell

The Shocking History of the Jesuits (The Society of Jesus)

King James I of England: The King The Vatican Could Not Kill

Oliver Cromwell: The Last King of England

The Hidden Truth About Freemasonry, The Catholic Church, And The Illuminati

Bible Prophecy Made Simple For Serious Students of Scripture

Did The Catholic Church Order Abraham Lincoln's Assassination?

Is Calvinism And The Doctrines of Grace Biblical?

The Book of Genesis Commentary (Chapters 1-11)

Watchman Nee, Witness Lee, and Living Stream Ministry: A Critical Analysis of Their Identity as Cult or Church

What Is Speaking In Tongues And Is It Still For Today?

Ephesians Bible Commentary

The Book of Romans Commentary